WITNESS AND REVELATION
IN THE GOSPEL OF J

ALTHOUGH THIS STUDY witness of and to Jesus as recorded in the Gospel of John, emerges as the focal point of all divine and saving revelation, it covers a wide range of revealed truth. Beginning with the Old Testament background Dr. Boice shows how "witness" came to stand as a term for "revelation", and how this concept was carried over into the N.T., coming to full expression the life, death and resurrection of the historical Jesus Christ, and finding its continuing evidence in the combined and inspired teachings of the apostles enshrined in the New Testament Scriptures. In their "witness" the Spirit of God bears testimony to the truth "revealed" in Jesus to its saving power to those who "hear" the witness, "see" the revelation, and believe unto eternal life.

Dr. Boice studied at Harvard and at Princeton and is a Doctor of Theology of the University of Basel. He is pastor of the Tenth Presbyterian Church of Philadelphia and ministers weekly on the coast-to-coast Bible Study Hour radio programme.

OTHER TITLES IN THIS SERIES:

WITNESS AND REVELATION IN THE GOSPEL OF JOHN

James Montgomery Boice, B.D., D. Theol.

THE PATERNOSTER PRESS

ISBN: 0 85364 099 8

All Scripture quotations in this volume,
unless otherwise stated, are from the Revised
Standard Version of the Bible, copyright 1946
and 1952 by the Division of Christian Educa-
tion of the National Council of Churches of
Christ in the U.S.A., and are used by permission.

AUSTRALIA:
Emu Book Agencies Pty., Ltd.,
511 Kent Street, Sydney, N.S.W.

CANADA:
Home Evangel Books Ltd.,
25 Hobson Avenue, Toronto, 16

NEW ZEALAND:
G. W. Moore, Ltd.,
3 Campbell Road, P.O. Box 24053,
Royal Oak, Auckland 6

SOUTH AFRICA:
Oxford University Press,
P.O. Box 1141, Thibault House,
Thibault Square, Cape Town

Made and Printed in Great Britain for
The Paternoster Press Paternoster House
3 Mount Radford Crescent Exeter Devon
by Cox & Wyman Limited Fakenham

TO
THE FAITHFUL AND TRUE WITNESS
THE BEGINNING
OF THE CREATION OF GOD

CONTENTS

Preface

When the author began this study as part of his doctoral work at the University of Basel, Switzerland, he expected to contribute to previous studies on the martyr question or to studies of the Church's witness. Instead, he soon found that references to "witness" in the Fourth Gospel refer only in a secondary sense to the testimony of believers and have almost nothing to do with the development of the word *martys* in the second century to denote one who had died for Jesus Christ. John's references to witness are concerned with revelation, the revelation of God to man in the historical Jesus and in the Scriptures, and with the verification of Christ's religious claims.

In the last century B. F. Westcott summarized the scope of the witnesses cited by the fourth evangelist in the course of the composition of the gospel by noting that the seven types of witness cover the whole range of the possible proof of religious truth—internal and external, personal and experiential. In some of its general outlines Westcott's perception of the scope of revelation in John has been vindicated in the following examination.

In the present study the witness of Jesus Christ emerges as the focal point of all divine and saving revelation. Revelation has its beginning in the Old Testament Scriptures mediated by the pre-incarnate Logos, comes to full expression in the life, death, and resurrection of the historical Jesus Christ, and has its final expression in the New Testament Scriptures representing the combined and inspired teachings of the historical apostolate. In their witness, which is the witness of the New Testament Scriptures, the Spirit of God bears testimony to the truth revealed in Jesus—to the salvation of those who believe and to the present and final judgment of those who reject the revelation.

John the Baptist, the signs, and the Scriptures bear an added witness to Jesus' claims, all being in a very real sense the direct and supernatural witness of the Father to the Son. These witnesses are themselves three modes of revelation.

The author is aware that John's references to witness are only one aspect of the Johannine theology. They need to be supplemented, as they have been in part in this study, by attention to other theological terms. At the same time, he believes that the witness terminology in John is much more important than has often been recognized and is vitally important for any investigation of the Johannine doctrine of revelation. The insights of the fourth evangelist also have a bearing on the doctrine of revelation in the New Testament (and in the Old Testament) generally.

I wish to express special thanks to Professor Bo Reicke of Basel, who directed the writing of the original version of this thesis and to Professor Oscar Cullmann, who served as *Koreferent* in presenting it to the Theological Faculty. I am also indebted to my wife, who shared in the discussion of these themes as well as in the laborious task of typing the manuscript and reading proof.

A section of chapter 5 (pp. 130-136) has already appeared as an article in *Christianity Today* and is reprinted by permission.

JMB

Philadelphia, Pa.

WITNESS AND REVELATION
IN THE GOSPEL OF JOHN

Chapter 1

Revelation and Witness

WITNESS AS A TERM FOR REVELATION

Today there is every reason to take a fresh look at the biblical view of revelation. An inquiry into the biblical understanding of the divine disclosure and into the biblical modes of expressing it is required, in the first place, by the challenge proffered to both systematic and biblical theology by Rudolf Bultmann of Marburg. By opting for an existential approach to Christianity in which the event of revelation is localized entirely in personal encounter and by basing this approach upon the alleged demands of biblical exegesis conceived as demythologizing, Bultmann has dislodged the doctrine of revelation from a setting entirely within the sphere of systematic theology (a setting which it had inevitably assumed in the studies of the crisis theologians), and has bound the theme itself ever closer to the concerns of New (and also Old) Testament exegesis. As a result of Bultmann's studies the meaning of revelation may no longer be considered without painstaking attention to the viewpoints, interests and vocabulary of the biblical writers.

A fresh inquiry into the biblical view of revelation is also required by the complex nature of purely systematic speculation. In systematic discussions the views of Karl Barth, Emil Brunner, Wolfhart Pannenberg, and others are so diffuse and so intricately interwoven that one is justified in believing that further progress can be made, not only by asking where the theologians leave off, but also where the Old and New Testaments begin, a course actually followed by many who give prominence to the historical character of the Christian revelation—Oscar Cullmann, H. Wheeler

Robinson, G. Ernest Wright, and others. The biblical scholar may well believe that the most profitable course for all reflection on revelation, the theme which systematic theology itself has thrust upon him, is that of listening to God's revelation itself, and this means listening to God's word in Scripture in which the Church finds her only infallible rule of faith and practice. G. C. Berkouwer, himself a systematician, agrees. "It is possible for the Church to speak of God's revelation only on the basis of God's Word in which she finds her norm and source for all her discussion of revelation." [1] And Barth, in the first volume of his *Church Dogmatics,* repeatedly affirms the same.

An investigation of the biblical understanding of revelation must be conditioned, however, by the fact that the writings of the Old and New Testaments consider the subject in a variety of contexts and with an unusual variety of terms. Berkouwer writes that "there is not one special, sacred word denoting God's revealing activity." [2] And his judgment is vindicated by the fact that in the New Testament alone the biblical writers employ such words as *apokalyptein, dēloun, phaneroun,* and *deiknynai* to speak explicitly of revelation, while reflecting the doctrine more obliquely through such terms as "word," "oracle," "Scripture," "it says" or "God says" and through such related concepts as inspiration (*theopneustos*), the law and the covenant. A firm recognition of the complexity of this doctrine and of the multiplicity of terms for expressing it has led Pannenberg to conclude, "In searching for clear statements of the self-revelation of God in the fate of Jesus in the New Testament writings, one must not keep too closely to the revelation terminology." [3] An adequate understanding of the biblical doctrine of revelation will be acquired only by a widespread examination of the many terms by which the characteristic biblical perspectives are conveyed.

In the Fourth Gospel an unusual word is used to speak of revelation. The word is "witness" or "testimony," and from the four related members of the word group in Greek (*martys, martyrein, martyria,* and *martyrion*) John has chosen two, the first of the cognates and the verb, to express his own understanding of the distinctive character of the Christian revelation. The evangelist has developed these two terms in such a way and in such a variety of contexts that in his gospel the witness terminology emerges from its original forensic setting, although without losing the valuable connotations of that setting, to express the significance of the divine disclosure in the Jesus of history and to relate the various aspects of the divine revelation—in the Scriptures, in the words of the prophets, in the acts and words of Christ, and in the operations of the Holy Spirit—to that primary revelation. By these terms John expresses a conception of revelation which can only be termed organic, a single, living revelation with a variety of forms, a conception in which the various expressions of revelation are united in Christ as their source, their content and their guiding principle. The words for witness in the Fourth Gospel are so important for expressing these ideas that it is questionable whether the Johannine view of revelation can be adequately perceived without an attempt to understand them.

Three additional factors add to the importance of this investigation. In the first place, the idea of witness itself is of major significance in the Johannine writings as is indicated both by the frequency with which the terms occur and by the variety of contexts in which the terms are found. This factor alone demands an investigation of the concept of witness in the gospel, quite apart from any relationship which the terms themselves may bear to revelation.

Secondly, if the witness terminology in John does have to do with revelation, this terminology is of exceptional significance owing to the fact that two of the most important words for the divine disclosure, *apokalyptein* and *dēloun,* do not occur in the pages of the gospel. This factor alone suggests that John's particular views may be expressed in concepts which one does not as a rule associate with revelation.

Finally, if the thesis which is expressed above is true, it is also true that the Johannine conception of witness is, religiously speaking, the highest and most important development of the word group to be found in Greek and Hebrew literature. In any language witness and testimony have a basically forensic denotation. In a higher connotative sense they may also have a reference to the gods, as to those who are mankind's witness ultimately and who represent the highest court of human appeal. But in Greek thought, as the gods diminish in importance (one must return to Homer for the sense just mentioned), the religious sense of the terms declines, and the testimony theme finds its final expression in reference to the philosopher and to the philosopher's witness. In Jewish thought, where the close connection between Jehovah and His people is never forgotten, the religious sense of the terms is fully developed, and the terms themselves express certain aspects of God's written revelation. John builds upon this foundation, arriving at new heights by virtue of his new understanding of the significance of the witness of Jesus Christ.

In spite of these truths and of the importance of the witness theme in general, the witness terminology has never been fully investigated in the Fourth Gospel in a way which points to and elucidates the significance of these terms for revelation. This is a surprising situation, but it is the direct result of two outstanding factors. The first is that the development of the witness terminology as a means for discussing revelation is peculiar to the traditional Johannine corpus—the gospel, the epistles and the Revelation—and has, therefore, been largely overlooked in general approaches to the witness word group. The second factor is that study of this distinctive Johannine contribution has been sidetracked by an intensive investigation on the part of scholars of the ways by which the substantive *martys* came to denote one who had died for his faith in Jesus Christ, a martyr. This last interest has so controlled the attention of most writers that the distinctive revelational connotation of the witness terminology in the Johannine writings has received little notice.[4]

THE OLD TESTAMENT BACKGROUND

To say that John's use of the witness terminology is unique in its conscious association of the terms *martyria* and *martyrein* with revelation does not mean that the author of the Fourth Gospel is entirely without precedent in doing so. In a general, but certainly a much less developed way, the themes which John develops and which he recasts on the basis of the new and determinative revelation which has come in Jesus Christ are already suggested in the pages of the Old Testament, especially in the religious witness of Isaiah and in the application of the substantive (the "testimonies") to the written law of God.

The idea of witness, of men and of God, plays a larger role in the Old Testament than might be imagined. The Hebrew verb *'ud,* from which are derived the substantive *'ed* and the cognates *'eduth* and *'edah,* means "to bear witness" in a court of law or before a council, "to call as a witness," "cause to witness," and "to solemnly affirm" (Hiphil). It usually occurs with the heightened implication of witnessing for or against a person or thing, and the Septuagint translates accordingly by *martyrein* plus the

prefixes *dia, epi* or *kata.* The substantive *'ed* denotes one who
testifies to a fact, thus "a witness" or "witnesses" whether false
or true, and can denote an object as well as a person. The cognates *'eduth* and *'edah* are both generally translated by *martyrion*
or *martyria.* The less frequent *'edah* occurs almost exclusively
as an appellative for the divine law or for the solemn charges of
Jehovah. *'Eduth* can mean this, too, but it is also used many
times in the stereotyped phrases: "the tabernacle [or tent] of the
testimony," "the ark of the testimony," and "the tables of the
testimony." In all of the above instances the forensic foundation
of the term is evident, but the application of the words to God
in many cases suggests a higher meaning in which the ideas of
testimony and revelation are combined.

In general the witness terminology in the Old Testament designates testimony rendered legally as before a court or council. The
largest number of instances use *'ed* to denote one who is called
before a council in order to establish a desired fact. For this
usage the basic texts are the legal maxims of Numbers 35:30;
Deuteronomy 17:6, 7 and 19:15 which require at least two witnesses to establish guilt in any criminal proceeding. In Leviticus
5:1; Numbers 5:13; Joshua 24:22 and Isaiah 8:2, it is particularly apparent that such witnesses must themselves be eye or ear
witnesses of the events in question. False witnesses are warned
severely and in Deuteronomy are threatened with the same fate
that they had devised for the one they wished to harm (Deut. 19:
16-19). An excellent illustration of such a retributive judgment
is afforded by the story of Susanna and her accusers in the apocryphal literature.

The Hebrew substantive may also denote one who by his
presence at a contract or an agreement becomes a witness for
the future for the things determined (Jer. 32:6-44; Ruth 4:9-11).

There are two ways in which the witness terminology of the
Old Testament builds upon this foundation in beginning to approach the full conception of testimony as God's commands or
revelation. The first is that in many instances the substantive *'ed*
is applied to things as well as people, making them, by what may
be called their lasting character, abiding evidences for an event
or an agreement, not only between men but between man and
God. The second is the poetic conception that pictures God in
a legal proceeding with Israel and with the heathen nations.

A few illustrations will make the first conception clear. In the classic passage of Genesis 31:43-53, Jacob and Laban erect a heap of stones as a witness (*gal'ed* and *sahadutha,* verse 47) to a contract to divide their possessions and to live in separate lands. Here there can be no interest in a subjective witness of the stones. They serve as a future reminder, a lasting evidence of the agreement reached between Jacob and Laban. As such they stand as a witness, not only between Jacob and Laban (verses 44 and 48), but also in the sight of God (verse 50) and in this way become symbolic of the presence of God at the agreement. A nearly identical case occurs twice in the book of Joshua, first, of an altar erected on the east bank of the Jordan as a reminder to the tribes that settled there that they were part of the confederation which settled Canaan (Josh. 22:27, 28, 34; cf. Isa. 19:20) and, second, of the great stone which Joshua erected as a witness to what God had spoken to the people through Joshua. "Behold, this stone shall be a witness against us; for it has heard all the words of the LORD which he spoke to us; therefore it shall be a witness against you; lest you deal falsely with your God" (Josh. 24:27).

In the apocryphal literature the same idea survives (as in Wisdom of Solomon 10:7 and other passages), and Moore cites a rabbinic document for an amusing exaggeration of the principle. In the tractate Sanhedrin 20c "Solomon, who multiplied wives, horses, silver and gold, contrary to Deuteronomy 17:17, eradicated the letter *yōd* in *l' yrbh* [thus changing the verb from a Hiphil imperfect to a Qal imperfect and altering the sense from a warning against multiplying possessions to a factual statement that they had been so multiplied]; the *yōd* became his accuser, and the Book of Deuteronomy prosecuted the case before God." [5]

The other type of approach to a specific religious witness terminology in the Old Testament is localized in two passages from Isaiah:

> Let all the nations gather together, and let the peoples assemble. Who among them can declare this, and show us the former things? Let them bring their witnesses to justify them, and let them hear and say, It is true. "You are my witnesses," says the LORD, "and my servant whom I have chosen . . . I, I am the LORD, and besides me there is no savior. . . . You are my witnesses," says the LORD (Isa. 43:9-12).

> Thus says the LORD, the King of Israel and his Redeemer,
> the LORD of hosts; "I am the first and I am the last; besides
> me there is no god. Who is like me? Let him proclaim it,
> let him declare and set it forth before me. . . . you are my
> witnesses! Is there a God besides me? There is no Rock; I
> know not any" (Isa. 44:6-8).

In these verses Jehovah appears with the peoples of the nations
in what can only be described as a legal proceeding, the object
of which is to establish recognition of His claims to be the only
and the sovereign God. In this proceeding all nations are called
upon to witness, but the decisive testimony is to be rendered by
Israel, which has observed His omnipotence and has experienced
His call and preservation. This is a religious witness. The object
to be affirmed is a religious truth, and the testimonies involved
are those of a spiritual and historical experience.[6]

For a religious witness in the Old Testament which really approaches the meaning of revelation, however, one must move beyond the citation of objects as witnesses and the somewhat poetic
description of God in legal proceeding with the people of the
nations in Isaiah to texts in which God Himself is said to testify
and to cases in which "*the* testimony" (as the definitive embodiment of God's spoken words) is applied to the Mosaic law.

God is described as a witness in a number of instances which
vary little from Paul's characteristic appeal to God in solemn
verification of the veracity of a statement (cf. Rom. 1:9; II Cor.
1:23; Phil. 1:8; I Thess. 2:5, 10). He is witness between Jacob
and Laban in Genesis 31:50, to the innocence of Samuel in
I Samuel 12:5 and to the future obedience of Israel in Jeremiah
42:5. The same idea is present in Job's appeal to a witness in
heaven (Job 16:19) where the correct rendering of the text by
the Revised Version as "Even now, behold, my witness is in
heaven, and my record is on high" makes explicit the identification of the witness with God.

There is also the witness of Jehovah through the prophets (II
Kings 17:13, 15; Neh. 9:29, 30, 34) which is a sure description
of prophetic revelation. It is in this sense that the witness must
be understood even when it is only the prophets themselves who
are said to testify (II Chron. 24:19; Neh. 9:26; Amos 3:13) or
when the words come through an intermediary such as the "angel
of the Lord" (Zech. 3:6). These testimonies involve the divine

command or statutes, which are to be received and obeyed simply because they do come from God and not from man.

The application of witness to the law is very frequent in the Old Testament. The largest number of instances relate to the wilderness tabernacle of the wandering nation and to the ark which occupied the central place within the Holy of Holies—"the tabernacle [or tent] of the testimony" (Ex. 38:21 and others), "the ark of the testimony" (Ex. 25:22 and others), "the tables of the testimony" (Ex. 31:18 and others) and "the veil of the testimony" (Lev. 24:3). In addition, there are a number of cases in the Pentateuch where the word occurs alone, denoting either the ark or the tables of the testimony. It would seem from these texts that the primary reference is to the stone tables containing the ten commandments which God had instructed Moses to place within the ark, for it is more probable that the ark derived its name from what it was designed to hold than that the tables derived their designation from the ark. The tables therefore become God's testimony in a special sense, namely as an objective and written revelation.

In the books of I and II Kings, I and II Chronicles and the Psalms both *'eduth* and *'edah* are often used in the phrase "his testimonies" and denote the whole of the written law, as is evident from the parallel terms—statutes, ordinances, decrees—with which they occur. In addition to these instances there are three examples of the phrase in Deuteronomy 4:45; 6:17 and 20, and it is probably the book of the written law which is intended in II Kings 11:12 (par. II Chron. 23:11) where the "testimony" is said to have been put into the hands of the young King Joash at his coronation.

With these texts the student comes to the third and last stage of the development of a specifically religious testimony in the Old Testament. The first stage occurs when God Himself is described as a witness either for or against an event or nation. This testimony is only a heightening of witness in its basically forensic connotations. The second stage deals with revelation itself both through the prophets and in the associations with the tabernacle and ark of the testimony. The third application of the terminology restricts it to the written law. Thus does the passive witnessing of God of men's deeds move to the active witness of God Himself and from thence to the descriptive designation of His commandments.

From this point on caution must be exercised against two conceivable errors. First, an overemphasis may be placed upon the written law as the crucial concept in the testimony of God in the Old Testament, that is, upon the objective revelation to the suppression of the active and consequently subjective element in the witnessing of God. Second, an equally erroneous negation of the objective element may be made, as if God's communion with the people did not have as one of its objects the establishing of a written revelation or could not be present in and through such a revelation after it had been established.

The ark of the testimony was certainly the place in which God was considered actively to meet His people. This is evident from the stories of the meetings which men had with God before the ark (Num. 7:89; 17:1-11) and from the specific statement that God would speak to Moses from above the mercy-seat (Ex. 30:6). It is interesting moreover to note the frequent occurrence in the Old Testament of the phrase *'ohel mo'ed,* "the tabernacle of *meeting"* (Ex. 27:21; 29:4; 33:7; Lev. 1:1, 3; Num. 11:16; 12:4; Deut. 31:14; Josh. 18:1; 19:51; I Sam. 2:22; I Kings 8:4, par. II Chron. 5:5; I Chron. 9:21; 23:32; II Chron. 1:3, 6, 13), which is nearly synonymous and interchangeable with the phrase "the tabernacle of the testimony" and emphasizes more strongly perhaps than the idea of testimony the active nature of the divine revelation.

At the same time, however, the objective element is strong, as is indicated by a certain focusing of interest upon the stone tables of the law and by the later development of "testimony" to designate the written law without reference to the tabernacle or to the ark as the place of meeting. It is certainly not irrelevant to this aspect of the argument that in the Septuagint both "the tabernacle of meeting" and "the tabernacle of the testimony" are rendered by the identical phrase (*ē skēnē tou martyriou*) which would seem to indicate that by the time of the Christian era at least and for some time before both Hebrew phrases were regarded as stereotyped descriptions of the tabernacle and ark in which the verbal element cannot be supposed to have played an important role. As many Old Testament scholars have observed, in Hebrew thought the presence and personal activity of God are not negated by a written revelation. The written law and the divine speaking belong together. They interpret one another and exist as equally significant aspects of the self-revelation of God. It is the merit of the word "testimony" as applied to the divine revelation that it is particularly suggestive of both these connotations.[7]

When this fundamental unity is fully perceived, it will also be evident that something more must be said about revelation as personal testimony and as written testimony than has been noticed previously. In the first place, it will be seen that it is not legitimate to minimize the value of written revelation on the ground of its being dated, fossilized or as being unable to speak to *me*, as is often done in contemporary discussions. God's words take written form, but even as such they remain God's words and retain their personal and active character. The Hebrew conception of a written revelation does not depart from the Hebrew idea of a personal God, and for this reason in Hebrew thought the written, Mosaic law does not lose the elements of personal obedience to God and of human responsibility which the personal relationship entails. At the same time the idea of a written law balances the idea of a personal encounter. The personal encounter is not without and does not operate without a norm. That God's revelation is personal does not mean that it is variable, as if two people could in the same circumstances receive basically contradictory revelations of the divine will. The variable, human element is only one aspect of the total process of revelation. The controlling factors are the unchangeable character and abiding purposes of God, and these may be placed in written form simply because and not in spite of the fact that they are abiding and unchangeable.

By its association with this personal and at the same time objective character of biblical revelation, witness in the Old Testament not only influences but is also influenced by the conception of a self-revealing God. When described as testimony, revelation becomes that which is humanly heard, believed and written down as distinct from a vision or a mystical perception in the tradition of the oracles of Greece. When testimony is described as revelation the forensic aspects of the word group fall away or at least retreat into the background, and the self-testimony of the sovereign God, pictured perhaps by the language of the court, but ultimately transcendent and independent of any human witness or support, remains. God's revelation is *His* revelation; His witness is *His* witness. He is self-authenticating. For in the imagined legal process it is God Himself who is ultimately both witness and advocate, both jury and judge.

Chapter 2

Witness in the Fourth Gospel

THE IDEA OF WITNESS IN JOHN

To the careful student of the Fourth Gospel there can be little doubt that the apostle John reflected long and perceptively on the idea of the Christian witness. In the first place, the lexical data point to this conclusion. Unlike the rest of the New Testament, in which the witness terminology appears at random and with the exception of Luke and Acts without appearance of a technical development, the words for witness are carefully selected in John and occur with a frequency which is itself worthy of notice.

The verb *martyrein,* which is found thirty times in the rest of the New Testament, occurs forty-seven times in the Johannine corpus—thirty-three times in the Fourth Gospel, ten times in I and III John and four times in Revelation. Thus, the Johannine books account for three-fifths of the occurrences of the verb in the New Testament. And the instances in the gospel alone appear with a frequency eleven times that of the Synoptics (three instances), three times that of Acts (eleven instances) and four times that of the Pauline epistles (eight instances). A more remarkable situation holds for *martyria,* one of two cognates meaning "testimony." In this case there are only thirty-seven instances in the New Testament, but the gospel of John accounts for fourteen, I and III John for seven, and Revelation for nine more. By contrast the word is completely missing from Matthew, occurs three times in Mark, and is present only once in Luke. The Johannine books thus account for thirty of the thirty-seven occurrences.

At the same time it must be observed that words which occur at random throughout the rest of the New Testament are apparently avoided by the writer of the Fourth Gospel. The most obvious case is the word for a witness, *martys*. Acts shows a particular understanding of the office of a witness and uses it thirteen times, and the rest of the books employ it now and then. But John does not. In place of the substantive the gospel uses a participle of the verb, thereby denoting God the Father (5:32, although perhaps the Baptist instead), the Samaritan woman (4:39), and the beloved disciple (21:24). *Martyrion,* the other cognate meaning testimony (in the sense of formally subscribed evidence or proof), occurs at random in the Synoptics, Acts, and the Pauline letters, but it too is avoided by John. And so are the less common words with heightened meanings which are often employed with vigor by the apostle Paul. In fact, with the exception of five instances of the word *martys* in Revelation and one occurrence of *martyrion* in a phrase which is taken over directly from the Septuagint (Rev. 15:5), only *martyrein* and *martyria* occur in the entire five books of the traditional Johannine corpus. At the same time it must be noticed that John uses these two words with a frequency so much in excess of the other New Testament books that the limitation in word choice must be explained by a conscious selection rather than by ignorance or neglect.

To assign a specific reason to John's neglect of *martys* and *martyrion* in preference for the verb and *martyria* is precarious, but it is not unwarranted, even at this point, to note that the Johannine selection suggests a concern for the actual witness-giving, the event, as opposed to the subject matter submitted as an evidence or proof. It would be a serious mistake to infer from this that John is uninterested in evidence, for various evidences are offered, and in some measure the place of the cognate *martyrion* is taken by the Johannine emphasis upon the signs. Nevertheless, it is true to say that the evangelist's emphasis seems to lie on the event instead of the conditions. "According to John witness is clearly an event, not a relationship, a deed rather than a thing."[1] At the very least John wishes to call attention to this aspect of the testimony.

The second fact suggestive of a conscious reflection on the meaning and scope of the Christian witness by the author of the Fourth Gospel is a diversity of contexts and associations in which the two words used by John occur. Seven types of witness are to be found throughout the gospel. And these, as Westcott observes correctly in his commentary, are arranged to cover the whole range of the possible proof of religious truth. The following are prominent.

1. The witness of John the Baptist. It is remarkable that in this gospel the Baptist seems to be introduced solely for the sake of his testimony to Jesus Christ (1:8, 15, 34; 3:26; 5:33) and entirely without reference to his ministry as a preacher of righteousness. His testimony is to the light (1:7) and involves both the confession of his own limited role (1:19 ff.) and the proclamation of the sign given to him at Christ's baptism (1:32). In chapter five Christ acknowledges this witness (verse 33) while at the same time speaking of a witness which exceeds that of the Baptist (verse 36).

2. The testimony of other human witnesses. The first of these witnesses is given by the Samaritan woman (4:39), who is followed by a multitude which had witnessed the raising of Lazarus (12:17), the special witness of the disciples (15:27), and the testimony of the eyewitness of the crucifixion, who is presumably the beloved disciple (19:35; 21:24). To these may rightly be added the witness of the blind man in chapter nine, although the word "witness" does not occur in this account. The testimony of these observers is partial. It is only a witness to the facts which they can verify. But it is particularly impressive simply because it does not exceed their respective limitations.

3. The witness of the Father. The testimony of the Father is emphasized by Jesus as the proper witness to Himself (5:32, 37), although the sense in which this witness is intended is not readily apparent. It is most probable that this witness is manifest in various ways, among them certainly the testimony of the works of Christ and of the Scriptures; and it is likely that the Father's witness is to be perceived as well in the testimony of John the Baptist. Jesus' claim to the Father's testimony is reiterated in 8:18.

4. The witness of Jesus Christ. Christ's testimony depends upon His special knowledge of Himself, His origin and His destiny (8:13-18), and is valid because that knowledge is complete and because the witness is born in perfect conjunction with the Father with whom Christ experienced an immediate and intimate communion. Before Pilate Christ provides a significant summation of His own witness by terming it a witness to the truth (18:37; cf. 3:11).

5. *The witness of Christ's works.* John calls the works of Jesus "signs" (*sēmeia*), and these are to be seen, not only in the recorded miracles, but in all aspects of Christ's life and conduct. Jesus says that the works are given Him to do by the Father and that they bear witness to Himself that the Father has sent Him (5:36; 10:25). The witness of the works is therefore preparatory for belief. In some measure it is secondary to the witness of the words (14:11), but nowhere in the gospel is the witness of the works disparaged. In fact, the works are even to be continued by the disciples after Christ's return to the Father, and they will perform greater works than He (14:12-14).

6. *The witness of the Scriptures.* In Christ's definitive defense of His religious claims in chapter five, the Scriptures are explicitly cited as bearing direct testimony to His person (verse 39).

7. *The witness of the Holy Spirit.* The testimony of the Holy Spirit, which in the nature of the narrative is cited late in the gospel and which will operate only after Christ has returned to heaven, carries the citation of various testimonies into the subjective experience of the believer. The Spirit will not testify regarding Himself. He has the task of progressively unfolding the significance of Christ's life, death, and resurrection to the disciples and to the generation of believers which are to follow them (16: 13, 14). In his first epistle John highlights the Spirit's testimony by the observation that "the Spirit is the witness, because the Spirit is the truth" (I John 5:7).

From this listing of the types of witness in John a third point emerges which also points to sustained reflection by the author of the gospel on the subject of the Christian witness. It has been observed that seven different kinds of witness are listed in the gospel: the witness of John the Baptist, the testimony of other human witnesses, the witness of the Father, the witness of Jesus Christ, the witness of Christ's works, the witness of the Scriptures, and the internal testimony of the Holy Spirit. But all of the seven are not equal. Some witnesses are partial. Some are dependent on the others. It would be possible to make a meaningful distinction between those witnesses which are divine in origin and therefore primary and those which are human, secondary, and responsive. This is the course followed, for instance, by van Pelt in the article on "Witness" for the *Hastings Dictionary of Christ and the Gospels.* In the Fourth Gospel itself, however, a division is indicated, not between the divine and the human testimony, however valid that distinction may be, but between the testimony of Jesus Christ and all other testimony, including that of the Father and the Holy Spirit. With the possible exception of Christ's own testimony, all of the testimony in the gospel points exclusively to Him. And even in Christ's case, Jesus bears witness to Himself (8:14), as well as testifying to the Father (3:31-34) and to the truth (18:37), expressions which must ultimately be understood to be synonymous (14:6, 9). With characteristic attention to detail Strathmann has noted that of the thirty instances of the word *martyria* in the Johannine corpus twenty-seven deal specifically with the essential nature and meaning of Jesus Christ, and Brox observes that with only a few exceptions of neutral word sense, the forms of the verb allude exclusively to Christ's person or to the meaning of His coming as the object. For this reason the meaning of Christ's person and the significance of His testimony are determinative for the Johannine conception of the Christian witness.

Christ's testimony is central for another reason as well. The witness of Jesus is not of the same kind as the witness of men to Him, or even, although this relationship must be more carefully defined later, of the divine verification of His ministry and person by the Father through the works and the Scriptures. In John Christ is the witness par excellence. He is the only one to have Himself observed the Father (1:18; 6:46), and as a result all human witness, and even the witness of the works and the Scripture, may only be a witness to the Father and to heavenly reality through Him. Christ's witness, as the witness of the Son of God, involves an immediate and undistorted apprehension of divine reality. And as such it is only truly perceived when it is accepted as the divine testimony of God to Himself. The Father witnesses in Christ, and this witness is unique. In this sense Barth's observation is correct when he writes: "the original and proper witness to God is no man, but God himself. . . . God alone must speak of God; for God only God suffices." [2] The Johannine interest in witness can never be separated from this characteristic perception and the resulting theological orientation.

From the foregoing it will already have become apparent that something more than mere reflection is involved in the Johannine idea of witness. There is more than an interest in witness. There is a theological interest, and the witness so considered is no mere witness in an original forensic sense but a religious witness, involving the presentation, verification and acknowledgment of the claims of Jesus Christ. Theology involves a delineation and a definition of concepts, an investigation of the areas in which the concepts apply or may be expected to apply, and a careful relating of the uncovered areas to one another. All of these conditions are met in the Johannine handling of the witness terminology. In the Fourth Gospel the implications of *martyrein* and *martyria* are developed in a variety of contexts, and the witnesses thus delineated are clustered carefully and with forethought about the primary and only autonomous testimony of the Lord.

In summary, John reflects as a theologian upon the nature and meaning of the Christian witness, and the resulting religious witness attains a peak of development in the Fourth Gospel which is unparalleled in the remainder of the New Testament sources.

LUKE-ACTS AND HEBREWS

With the exception of the Johannine books, it is only in the Lukan literature and in Hebrews that the student of the New Testament encounters a technical use of the witness terminology which appreciably exceeds the popular usage, a usage reflected widely in Matthew and Mark and in the Pauline letters.[3]

In Acts one finds human witness as a recruiting confession of the facts concerning Jesus Christ. In a more restricted sense one also finds *martys* designating a member of a body of chosen men especially commissioned to bear witness. This is a new departure. And the impetus toward it is found in the Lukan version of the great commission: "You shall be my witnesses" (Acts 1:8) and "You are witnesses of these things" (Luke 24:48). The witnesses are those who fulfill a twofold qualification. First, they must have a special knowledge of the events of Christ's life, death and resurrection (Acts 2:22-32; 10:36-40; 13:23-31), and second, they must have been chosen by the resurrected Lord to testify about Him (Acts 1:2, 24; 10:41). To complete the number of the twelve, selection was made from among those whose knowledge was both firsthand (Luke 1:2) and complete (Acts 1: 21, 22). In later declarations the emphasis seems to have fallen largely upon the necessity of having seen the resurrected Lord together with the resulting ability to testify to the fact of the resurrection (Acts 2:32; 3:15; 5:30-32; 10:39-41; 13:30, 31).

A certain flexibility of definition is required, however, by Luke's application of *martys* to Paul in Acts 22:15 and 26:16 and to

Stephen, the first martyr, in Acts 22:20. These verses have presented difficulties in that Paul was certainly not a companion of Christ during His earthly ministry, and there is no record of Stephen either having been a disciple or of having received a call to apostleship. Strathmann, for instance, has considered the reference to Paul to be artificial and not wholly successful, and Cerfaux has attempted to force a distinction between the terminology used of the twelve and that which is used of Paul.[4] It is certainly no accident, however, that both qualifications for apostleship are stressed in Acts 22:14, 15—"The God of our fathers *appointed* you to know his will, to *see* the Just One and to *hear* a voice from his mouth [his voice]; for you will be a witness for him to all men of what you have *seen* and *heard*"—and Luke undoubtedly intends to teach that for the validity of his apostleship Paul's Damascus vision was equivalent to the eyewitness experience of the Twelve. In this he certainly reflects Paul's own claim to be the last of the apostles (I Cor. 9:1; 15:8). Luke neither contradicts his customary usage nor coins a new conception. He extends the definition to include the special case of Paul.

The case of Stephen is more difficult because apparently both requirements for apostleship are lacking. Nevertheless, Campenhausen finds both of them in Stephen's vision of the exalted Christ (Acts 7:55, 56) and considers the testimony of Stephen to be rendered to that sight.[5] In support of this argument it is useful to note that in the context of Paul's speech the designation of Stephen as a witness occurs only a few verses after the recounting of Paul's own vision and of his own call to the apostolate. And within the context one can easily argue that the use of the word is identical. It is far more likely, however, that Luke merely departs from his own technical usage of the term, referring simply to Stephen's verbal testimony. This would be particularly appropriate in view of Stephen's reputation for eloquence (Acts 6:10).[6]

At all events, the restriction of the word *martys* by Luke to designate those who have a firsthand knowledge of the resurrected Lord and have been called by Him to witness to the world is unaffected by a variation in the case of Stephen. Because of this knowledge and of this special calling the disciples become witnesses in a special and, with the exception of Paul and possibly a few others, an exclusive sense. The disciples do not become witnesses through the preaching. They are authorized to preach because they have been chosen as witnesses.

In a less ambitious way the epistle to the Hebrews comes quite close to the Johannine usage, for it contains two parallels to characteristic Johannine ideas; first, the witness of Scripture to Christ's coming and to the significance of His ministry (Heb. 2:6; 3:5; 7:8, 17; 10:15), and, second, the witness of the Father to spiritual truths through signs and wonders (Heb. 2:4; cf. Acts 14:3). In chapter eleven *martyrein* is used of the Old Testament heroes who have received divine testimony of a good character through faith in God (verses 2, 4, 5, 39). In such cases either God the Father or God the Holy Spirit is considered the subject of a moral judgment to which the ultimate appeal of the apostle Paul—"God is my witness"—provides a parallel.

The Theology of Witness in John

To claim that the apostle John has reflected as a theologian upon the idea of religious witness and has constructed his presentation of testimonies to point exclusively to Jesus Christ is to introduce a host of questions. How do the testimonies of men and the testimony of the Father relate to the witness of the Lord? What is the significance of Christ's witness? If John has considered Christ's witness from a theological perspective, just what aspect of theology is involved when he deals with the testimony of Jesus? And when this question is answered, what does the nature of Christ's witness reveal about this aspect of theology? If Christ's witness were a deed witness, for instance, the witness would presumably be centered in the cross, and the aspect of theology with which John deals would be the doctrine of salvation, soteriology. To link the witness of Jesus with His death on the cross might then signify that the cross is to be understood as the ultimate evidence of the newly established relationship between men and God. Such a development of the witness idea would be valid. But, in point of fact, this is not the course followed by the fourth evangelist. John does not relate the witness of Jesus to the thought of His atonement nor to a specific office by which the facts of His ministry are to be established, as Luke does by the development of the normative witness of the apostles. For John the witness of Jesus is *revelation,* and the witnesses which cluster about it are expressions by the evangelist of those aspects of revelation which concern the subjective appropriation and objective verification of religious truth. The answers to the preceding questions will be found in this context in the following chapters.

The evangelist is most explicit in his association of the witness of Jesus with revelation in chapter three. Here Christ's testimony is cited in a context in which the superior knowledge of Jesus (possibly also of the disciples or of the Old Testament prophets as suggested by the plural verb forms of verse 11) is contrasted with the earth-bound vision of Nicodemus, the representative ruler of the Jews. In the first half of the chapter Jesus claims to have testified of what He has seen in heaven, although He lays great stress upon the fact that Nicodemus' lack of comprehension has prevented the revelation of things which are truly heavenly (verse 12). Jesus has a comprehensive knowledge of these things because He has descended from heaven and will yet return to it. The idea of Christ's special knowledge occurs again at the end of the chapter, but in these verses it is broadened beyond the immediate context of the conversation with Nicodemus, in which the emphasis falls upon the fact that Christ spoke only "earthly" things to the Jewish ruler, to an expression of the fullness of revelation contained in the testimony of the incarnate Lord. "He who comes from above is above all; he who is of the earth belongs to the earth, and of the earth he speaks; he who comes from heaven is above all. He bears witness to what he has seen and heard. . . . For he whom God has sent utters the words of God, for it is not by measure that he gives the Spirit" (verses 31, 32, 34). Similar expressions of Christ's role as a revealer occur throughout the gospel. In the presence of Pilate, as has already been noted, Jesus further describes the purpose of His own ministry as a coming to earth to bear witness to the truth (18:37).

The association of revelation with the witness of Jesus Christ is not really surprising in light of the emphasis on the idea of revelation which occurs through the gospel. Indeed the gospel of John might be called the gospel of revelation, the revelation of Jesus Christ, to borrow the phrase, although in a different sense, by which the apocalypse is commended to its readers. The most important word for revelation in the New Testament vocabulary, *apokalyptein* ("to uncover," "to reveal"), does not occur in John, and neither does *dēloun* ("to reveal," "to make clear," "to explain"). But there are many examples of other words for revelation as well as many concepts which deal with the subject by metaphor or by implication.

The first specific use of a word for revelation occurs in 1:31 in the Baptist's declaration: "For this I came baptizing with water, that he might *be revealed* to Israel." As a historical restatement of the themes of the prologue, this verse sets the context for the subsequent narration. The verb in this instance is *phaneroun* ("to reveal," "to make known" and to a lesser extent "to show"). This word is repeated with a similar meaning, although in a context of unbelief, when the brothers of Jesus challenge Him to reveal Himself to the people at Jerusalem (7:4); and after the resurrection Jesus is on two occasions said to have revealed Himself to the disciples (21:1 and 14). In 2:11, shortly after the statement of the Baptist which is cited above, Jesus reveals His glory to the disciples through the changing of the water into wine at Cana. In the priestly prayer of John seventeen Jesus claims to have revealed the name of the Father to the twelve (verse 6).

The striking conception of making known the name—a clear reference to the significance of the Tetragrammaton in Judaism and to the awesome accounts of the revelation of the name of God in the Old Testament Scriptures (cf. Exodus 3:13-15 for the definitive example)—occurs again with the verb *gnorizein* ("to make known," "to reveal"). Christ says in the same prayer, "I made known to them thy name, and I *will make* it *known*" (verse 26). The same verb is used again in Christ's claim that "all that I have heard from my Father I *have made known* to you" (15:15). In most of these instances the reference is to a supernatural revelation, and in some of them the revelation is connected with the speaking of the words of God by Jesus and with His testimony of what He has seen and heard in heaven.

Another verb which sometimes speaks of revelation is *deiknynai* ("to show"). This word occurs seven times in the Fourth Gospel and eight times in the book of Revelation, referring always to an apocalyptical vision in the latter book. In the gospel it is generally used of something visible to the eye. Thus, Jesus *shows* His hands and side to the disciples after the resurrection (20: 20) and speaks on one occasion of the good works which had been *shown* to the Jewish rulers as a sign to them (10:32). In 2:18 the Jews ask to be *shown* a sign. A visible phenomenon, in this case a theophany, is also intended when Philip asks for a vision of the Father (14:8), and the reference is quite probably to the visible revelation of God's power in the world when Christ states that "the Father loves the Son, and *shows* him all that he himself is doing; and greater works than these will he *show* him, that you may marvel" (5:20). To this list can be appended a number of other words used metaphorically by John to express the revelation which is manifest in Christ. Such are the verbs "to send," "to send out," and "to come." The verbs "to hear," "to see," "to look at" and terms for "knowing," "perceiving," and "believing" often deal with human perception of the divine revelation.[7] Insofar as the instances of the words for revelation have to do with Jesus Christ, John deals with the words of God as they are declared to men by Christ and with the glory of the Father as that glory is revealed in the actions of the Son. John's understanding of the witness of Jesus moves hand in hand with these conceptions.

In the revelation of God's glory through the actions of His Son an element of objectivity is introduced into the idea of revelation in the Fourth Gospel which is further emphasized by the application of the witness idea to the role of Scripture in validating the witness of the Son. The witness with which John deals is not only spoken and not only acted out in history. It is also written. The Scriptures themselves bear witness to Jesus. And this is to say that John deals with the forms of witness in such a way that the idea of a written and a spoken revelation described thereby, and also of an objective and a subjective revelation, do not oppose one another but rather belong together as indispensable aspects of that one revelation which God by grace has made known to men and has focused in the person of His Son. In the ability to perceive a harmony in all of the facets of revelation, where certain philosophical evaluations of the subject would perceive a conflict, the evangelist echoes the Old Testament perception that the active speaking of God and the spoken revelation embodied in the law belong together. John's use of the witness terminology preserves the unity of revelation just as the Hebrew equivalents preserve the unity in the Old Testament sources.

The revelation which is present in the works of Christ and which is given objectively in the Old Testament Scriptures is not as complete as the revelation present in the person of the Lord, according to John, for it is not as personal. Jesus Christ has revealed the Father in the fullness of grace and truth (1:16, 17; 14:9), and this is not said in the same sense of the revelation given elsewhere. The works of Jesus are conducive to belief and are a verification by the Father of the claims of the Son, but it is quite possible for men to come to faith in Christ having never seen Him, or the signs which He performed (20:29; cf. 14:11). The Old Testament Scriptures are nowhere considered dispensable, but they are secondary insofar as their revelation is partial and in light of the fact that they point to Jesus rather than turn faith upon themselves (5:39, 40). Nevertheless, in neither case is this to deny that what is given for human contemplation in the signs and in the Scripture is revelation or that such an objective revelation is contradictory to the idea of a personal revelation, a personal speaking, a personal encounter as is emphasized in the Johannine portrait of Jesus Christ. It is significant that even with the new stimulus toward a personal, subjective revelation provided by the coming of Jesus, John does not depart from the Old Testament perception of a revelation which is at once both written and active, both spiritually expectant and yet not without a norm.

At the same time, although at one with the Old Testament perceptions, it is evident that John goes beyond the Old Testament expression of revelation by means of the witness terminology. John also deals creatively with human witness and with the subjective witness of the Spirit. In the first case, it cannot be said that the witness of men *is* revelation, even in a partial manner. What is at stake in this usage is a response to revelation—the acceptance of its validity and the communication of the revelation so received to others. The witness of the Spirit, as developed in the Fourth Gospel, relates to the subjective appropriation of the revelation which has been given to men in Christ and to the furtherance of human understanding of Christ's complete revelation of God in history. All of these types of witness are to be investigated in the following pages. What is to be noted at this point is that John's treatment of the idea of witness moves within the area of divine revelation, the verification of religious claims and the response of the individual to the revelation which is found in Christ. Because of its primary nature, the witness of Jesus and thus of His revelation must be considered first in the following discussion.

THE HISTORICAL CONTEXT

One other subject deserves notice by way of introduction. It must not be thought that John's reflection upon revelation and the subjects which are related to it is the product of a detached or academic speculation. There is an urgency about the Johannine interest in witness which must not escape notice, for it points an instructive finger to the historical situation of the apostle's day and to the ecclesiastical battle lines maintained at the time of the writing of the gospel.

By the end of the first century, when the gospel of John was written, the situation in the church was different from the early days of the Pauline mission and of the writing of the Synoptic gospels. The early random congregations were giving way to a more established institution, and with the fall of Jerusalem to the Roman armies under Titus the polemical interest, which before A.D. 70 had been largely directed against the Jews, now was increasingly directed toward the Gentiles. In John this changing outlook is reflected, quite independently of any ideas concerning witness, in the relative neglect of the theological relationship between faith and works and the attitude of Christians toward the Jewish law, which had occupied such a large place in the Pauline theology, and by a newly emerging sacramental interest and a concern for the problems of religious epistemology which would be of particular interest to a mind formed by the culture of the Hellenistic age.

At the same time the congregations had witnessed a remarkable growth of the Christian community. Reicke estimates that the number of confessing Christians and adherents of Christianity had multiplied eight times in the final third of the century, from 40,000 before A.D. 67 to 320,000 after the year A.D. 100,[8] and this factor alone was forcing the attention of the Gentiles upon the claims of Christianity. What was the evidence for this expanding faith? It was a time for analysis. An answer was required. And when John closes his gospel with the summation that "Jesus did many other signs in the presence of the disciples, which are not written in this book; but these are written that you may believe that Jesus is the Christ, the Son of God, and that believing you might have life in his name" (20:30, 31), he is conscious of having provided one. In such circumstances it was not only natural but imperative that John should have reflected upon the meaning of the Christian witness and that he should have attempted a more systematic presentation of the types of witnesses to which the early Church in imitation of Jesus Himself had been accustomed to refer.

The demands of the historical situation thus described as external to the Church were apparently reinforced by an internal emergency which also called for a restatement of the foundations of the faith. In the first epistle of John, in which the Johannine polemic against this danger is more explicitly expressed than in the gospel, even the casual reader will detect a vigorous offensive against a body of professing Christians who denied in some manner that Christ had come in the flesh, that Christ, the Son of God, was truly Jesus of Nazareth, the man. Such doctrines embodied a false spirituality and threatened the historical groundings of the faith. To John those who so taught were not in reality believers. One recalls the similar judgment of the apostle Paul against the Galatian legalizers (Gal. 1:6-9). The teachers to which John refers are antichrist (I John 2:18). They are of the spirit of error (I John 4:6) and deniers of God through their denial of a literal incarnation of His Son (I John 2:22, 23). According to Polycarp, who is quoted by Irenaeus, the leader for this movement was Cerinthus, a gnostic-like figure who taught an adoptionist Christology in which the spiritual and impassible Christ came upon Jesus at the baptism and deserted Him just before the crucifixion (*Adversus haereses,* 1:26). In the face of such statements and in regard to a subtle emphasis upon Christ's humanity throughout the gospel, it is surely not groundless to postulate, as many scholars have done, that a Docetic, gnostic-like threat existed within the Church for which the gospel and epistles were written.

It is difficult, of course, to speak of Gnosticism in connection with the Fourth Gospel. There are no Gnostic documents which can with any probability be dated before the first Christian century, and it is quite true that there was never one but several forms of Gnosticism in the Hellenistic world. Moreover, Gnosticism was a syncretistic and Hydra-headed faith. Many aspects of Gnosticism were shared by other religious systems, and as a result the errors against which John was fighting may have entered Christianity through other channels, as for example through an acquaintance with the mystery religions in which a belief in the mystical experience and the evil nature of the flesh and matter had played a starring role. All this is true and yet less probable. The fully developed Gnosticism of the second century had its roots in the first. And a gnostic-like movement, with its doctrine of salvation by esoteric knowledge and dualistic spiritualizing of the nature of God, would have posed a threat to the reality of Christ's historical existence and to the definitive nature of His earthly teaching intolerable to the author of the Fourth Gospel and the Johannine epistles. In the exigencies of the historical situation the idea of witness with its primary reference to the facts of Christ's life and with its emphasis upon the totality of revelation in its objective and subjective aspects would have provided John with an urgently needed as well as an authoritatively oriented reproof.

An unbelieving world required evidence for the religious claims of Jesus and His followers. And the deviation toward an esoteric religion within the Church required immediate correction by a reiteration of the historical groundings of the faith. In confronting such demands John has utilized the witness terminology for a careful re-examination of the historical claims of Christianity and for a theological restatement of its claim to and defense of revelation.

Chapter 3

The Witness of Jesus Christ

JESUS THE REVEALER

The witness of Jesus Christ in the Fourth Gospel arises quite naturally from the fact that Christ has been sent into the world by God. In all that He says and does Jesus is represented as one who is not of this earth, nor conditioned by the world's error and spiritual darkness, but as one who is from beyond the earth and who appears on earth as a life and light-giving messenger from God.

Christ's having been sent from God is not an idea which is unique to John. It is also present in the Synoptics and in the Pauline letters, although in these sources the theme takes a different form from that which is given to it by the fourth evangelist and exercises on the whole a less important role. In the gospel of Luke Christ speaks several times of his being sent, in each case associating the theme with His messianic functions (Luke 4: 18, 19, 43; cf. Mark 9:37; Matt. 10:40; 15:24 and Luke 9: 48). In Paul the idea of Christ's being sent occurs in the closest possible connection with God's eternal purpose in sending Christ for the salvation of the world (Rom. 8:3; Gal. 4:4). The sending derives its meaning from the themes of redemption and reconciliation.

In the Fourth Gospel there is also a theological perspective from which the sending of Jesus is considered, but it is difficult to feel that the evangelist depends upon the conception of Christ's being sent by God in either the Synoptics or in Paul.

In the first place, the theme is far too prevalent and, therefore, too important in John's narrative to be only an inconsiderate borrowing of an earlier usage. In the gospel the phrase "he (or the Father) who sent me" is found on the lips of Jesus twenty-three times (cf. also 13:16 where the phrase occurs in a proverb with a similar meaning), and the verb *apostellein* occurs seventeen times in phrases which refer to the Son's divine commission. Instances which speak from the human perspective of the fact that Christ has "come" are also numerous. Jesus is the one who "came down from heaven" (3:13; 6:33, 38, 42, 51); He "came from the Father [or God]" (8:42; 13:3; 16:27, 28, 30; 17:8); He is the one who has "come into the world" (3:19; 9:39; 11:27; 12:46; 16:28; 18:37). In the final discourses especially the emphasis shifts from the coming to the return (13:33; 14:1-4, 12, 28; 16:5, 7; 17:11, 13), and in 16:28 it is indicated in the Pauline manner that the coming and the return belong together (cf. also 13:3). "I came from the Father and have come into the world; again, I am leaving the world and going to the Father." These statements have little or no reference to the identification of Jesus as the Messiah as in the Synoptics or to the interpretation of His ministry in terms of the atonement as in the Pauline sources. Instead they refer to Jesus' ability to impart heavenly gifts and to speak the words of God to men. This is to say that in the Fourth Gospel the theme of Christ's being sent involves His identity as a *divine messenger* who is commissioned to enter this world for the sake of the revelation of the Father.[1] "No one has ever seen God; the only Son, who is in the bosom of the Father, he has made him known."

In the Fourth Gospel, however, the sending of Christ means more than the sending of a prophet as in Judaism or even of a divine messenger as was believed by the Greeks. Christ is not *a* messenger; He is *the* messenger. It must be remembered in considering this aspect of Christ's ministry that John the Baptist is also said to have been sent by God (1:6, 33; 3:28) and that the disciples are sent in their turn into the world (17:18; 20:21). But neither the Baptist nor the disciples exert a claim to independent revelation. They are sent only to bear witness to Jesus Christ. It is Christ alone who speaks and acts out of the fullness of His knowledge of the Father. The nature of His words (8:40; 12:49, 50) and the meaning of His works (5:19-21) are only comprehensible in relation to this divine commission.

There is a sense, of course, in which John represents Jesus as speaking only what He has seen and heard from the Father (3: 11; 7:16, 17) and, hence, as a dependent figure who does not possess a greatness of His own nor an independent revelation. But the imagined contradiction is superficial. In point of fact, it is precisely Christ's unique and total dependence on the Father which makes His being sent distinct from the sending of the prophets and which results in that utter oneness of mind and purpose which enables Jesus to claim that "he who has seen me has seen the Father" (14:9). With the motif of the sending John is not dealing with the messianic identity, the urgency of which passed with the fall of Jerusalem, nor with the atonement as the focal point of Jesus' mission, although the atonement is of great significance to John, but with a mediated revelation, and not only with a mediated revelation but with an absolute one such as would only be possible to the Son of God.

The fact that John represents Jesus as the absolute mediator of the divine revelation is indicated by other features of the Fourth Gospel also, although these have less direct bearing upon the idea of the witness of Christ than does His being sent from the Father. In a brief but excellent treatment of the idea of revelation in the gospel of John, Huber suggests three additional aspects of the narrative which also serve to absolutize Christ's function: 1) the idea of Christ's pre-existence, 2) the Christological nomenclature, and 3) the sharply emphasized antitheses between Christ and Moses, the gift of Christ and the Torah.[2] All of these features serve to highlight the uniqueness of the one on whom the gospel centers. What is said of Him may be said of no other. And, hence, His witness, while similar in outer form to that of men, is in reality a unique witness which is only possible for the unique and uniquely commissioned messenger of God.

It must be noted further in this same connection that in his presentation of Christ as the one whom God has sent, John does not permit his readers to think of Jesus as a mediator of revelation, or even as the ultimate mediator of revelation, in the same sense as the bearers of revelation known to the Hellenistic world. The ministry of Jesus derives its meaning from His source. And consequently it is not sufficient to regard Him merely as a revealer or *the* revealer. Jesus Christ must be acknowledged as *the revealer of the one true God,* the God of Israel, whom He designates as Father. John can therefore speak of Christ's having been sent by God as the supreme article of faith for those who

have been called by Him and who have come to know Him
for who He is. Such a faith is at once a faith in Jesus and in
Jehovah. In speaking to the Jews Jesus says that the work of
God is to "believe in him whom he has sent" (6:29; cf. 11:42),
and on one occasion the disciples reply to Christ that "we believe that you came from God" (16:30). In the priestly prayer
of John 17 Jesus notes twice that the disciples have believed
that "thou hast sent [didst send] me" (verses 8, 25) and prays
in a similar manner for those who will follow them in faith
(verses 21, 23). In the first epistle the congregation can likewise
affirm, "And we have seen and testify that the Father has sent
his Son as the Saviour of the world" (I John 4:14). For John
the recognition of the source from which Christ comes is synonymous with belief in Him and acceptance of His revelation, just
as, in an inverted manner, to recognize Christ, really to see Him,
is to see the Father (14:9).

In the dramatic and sometimes humorous story of the healing
of the blind man in chapter nine, John has included in his gospel
an illustration of belief which carefully combines the idea of faith
in Christ's person, stimulated by His works, and the element of
faith in regard to His coming from the Father. The highpoint of
the story is the dramatic contrast between the statement of the
Jewish rulers in verse twenty-nine and the confession of the man
who had been healed culminating in verse thirty-three. The Jews
argue from their own knowledge and authority, "We know that
God has spoken to Moses, but as for this man, we do not know
where he comes from." With irony the man born blind replies,
"Why, this is a marvel! You do not know where he comes from,
and yet he opened my eyes. . . . If this man were not from God,
he could do nothing." The man had been led by the healing of
his eyes to the spiritual perception that Jesus had come from God,
and as a consequence he was prepared to acknowledge Christ's
right to speak with an authority superior to that of the Mosaic
legislation. By contrast, the inability of the Jewish rulers to recognize Christ's coming, and hence His divine identity, led them to
reject both His miraculous works and His authoritative pronouncements. Belief in Christ's person and recognition of the source
from which He comes are closely bound together.

Thus, for John the revelation of Jesus Christ is the ultimate
and authoritative revelation, but it is so not only because it is a
perfect revelation, because Jesus revealed the Father in the full-

ness of grace and truth, but also and precisely because it is the revelation of the *Father,* Jehovah, the God of Israel, who is the one true God.

The bearing of the motif of Christ's being sent upon the idea of Christ's witness is, of course, already readily apparent, for if Christ's coming into the world is incomprehensible without reference to the Father who sent Him, so is His witness without a like reference to the Father who has spoken the words which Jesus comes to earth to utter. The student of the gospel finds it no surprise, therefore, that John never seems to tire of reiterating that Christ speaks, not on His own authority, but on the authority of the Father and in complete accord with what He has seen and heard in heaven. "Truly, truly, I say to you, we speak of what we know, and bear witness to what we have seen; but you do not receive our testimony" (3:11). "He who comes from above is above all. He bears witness to what he has seen and heard, yet no one receives his testimony. . . . For he whom God has sent utters the words of God" (3:31-34). "I can do nothing on my own authority; as I hear, I judge; and my judgment is just, because I seek not my own will but the will of him who sent me" (5:30). "My teaching is not mine, but his who sent me" (7:16). "I do nothing on my own authority but speak thus as the Father taught me" (8:28). "I speak of what I have seen with my Father" (8:38). "Now you seek to kill me, a man who has told you the truth which I heard from God" (8:40). "I have not spoken on my own authority; the Father who sent me has himself given me commandment what to say and what to speak. . . . What I say, therefore, I say as the Father has bidden me" (12:49, 50). "The words that I say to you I do not speak on my own authority; but the Father who dwells in me does his works" (14:10). "The word which you hear is not mine but the Father's who sent me" (14:24). And in the prayer of John 17 Jesus addresses the Father directly noting, "I have given them the words which thou gavest me" (verse 8) and "I have given them thy word" (verse 14).

By the witness of Jesus John deals with revelation, and not only with revelation, but with Jesus as the supreme revealer and that in such a way that the words of Jesus are incomprehensible without reference to the Father. Christ's words are the very words of God.

THE MESSIANIC CONSCIOUSNESS IN JOHN

In the development of the theme of Christ's being sent in John it has been generally presupposed, as has been done by the evangelist himself, that as the one who bears witness to what He has seen and heard in heaven Jesus is Himself keenly aware of the unique and intimate relationship in which He stands to God. As the personal mediator of the divine revelation Jesus must know Himself as such. And as the one who renders a perfect testimony Jesus must know Himself as the unique and perfect witness. This self-awareness is what has customarily been called, in discussion based largely upon the Synoptic gospels, the Messianic self-consciousness of Jesus. In the Fourth Gospel this self-consciousness is asserted even more strongly than it is in the Synoptics, although it is not concerned with Jesus' identity as the Messiah so much as with His knowledge of Himself as the revealer. In this gospel Christ's consciousness of a divine Sonship which belongs to Himself alone, His special knowledge of the Father, of men and of the divine plan for His ministry, and the special witness of Jesus to Himself which is developed in chapter eight all bear witness to Christ's awareness of His divine commission.

Many texts witness to Christ's awareness of His Sonship. Before the resurrection Jesus never refers to God as "our Father" but speaks instead of "my Father" or "the Father who sent me" (5:43; 6:57; 10:17, 18, 25; 12:49; 14:28, 31; 15:10). Such phraseology must indicate that Jesus is conscious of a special relationship to God possessed by Himself and by no other and which before the atonement and the consequent resurrection has no analogy in the relationship of other men to the one whom He calls Father. In many cases Jesus alone is declared to be the Son (5:19-27; 8:34-36). Jesus makes the significance of this relationship explicit in the claims that the one who has seen Him has seen the Father (14:6-11), that it is possible for God to be seen in all Christ's words and actions, and in the assertion of an essential unity between the Son and the Father in 14:10 (cf. 10:30): "I am in the Father and the Father in me." This latter expression serves as a *leitmotiv* for the narration (cf. 10:38; 13:31, 32; 17:21-23). The idea of a mutual knowledge between the Son and the Father is further expressed in 10:15 (cf. the same saying in Matt. 11:27) with the claim that "the Father knows me and I know the Father." And it is in the light of the knowledge of this unique relationship to God that Jesus declares Himself to be the object of faith and asserts that worship of Himself is worship given to the Father (5:23; 14:1).

It is a characteristic of the Fourth Gospel that Christ's consciousness of being the Son in this unique sense is traced, not only to His awareness of standing in a special relationship to God in His incarnate form, but also to His consciousness of having held the position of the Son of God from eternity. On this point Huber correctly observes: "The fourth evangelist views the relationship between Jesus and God as existing from eternity, unlike the case of men where it is initiated first through obedience to the 'Word.' " [3] Weiss concludes that while "Jesus sinks Himself in the origin of this peerless knowledge of God, He is conscious that it is to be traced to no point in his earthly life, and to no analogy in the religious experience of other messengers of God." [4]

The special relationship of Jesus as the Son of God to God the Father leads naturally by Christ's knowledge of this relationship to the theme of knowledge in general, a theme which is extensively developed in the gospel. The evangelist stresses repeatedly that Jesus' knowledge is a full and perfect knowledge—of the Father, as has already been noted, of men and of the work which has been given Him to do. Christ's knowledge of the Father is direct and absolute. In an article for *Biblica,* de la Potterie suggests, quite correctly, that *oida,* as used by John of Jesus, indicates "absolute" as opposed to "acquired" knowledge and is employed characteristically whenever Jesus speaks of knowing God: "The verb . . . indicates that Jesus knows divine things. Christ, and He alone, speaks in an absolute manner in referring to God." [5] Thus in 7:29 Jesus claims to know God because He came from God and was sent by Him. And in 8:55 Christ's knowledge of the Father is declared categorically on the same basis in opposition to the erroneous and sinful knowledge of the Jews. In other instances the knowledge of Jesus has for its object the internal thoughts and mental predispositions of the disciples, even to the degree of perceiving who it was who should betray Him (6:61, 64; 13:11). In 3:11 Christ's special knowledge of spiritual things is connected with the idea of testimony in the assertion: "We speak of what we know, and bear witness to what we have seen; but you do not receive our testimony." [6]

Christ's knowledge also extends to the works which the Father

has given Him to do, for Jesus' messianic consciousness is also
indicated in the gospel by the evangelist's marked attention to
the knowledge of His "time" and "hour." At the very beginning
of His ministry in Cana of Galilee, Jesus replies to His mother's
suggestion about the lack of wine by observing that "my hour
has not yet come" (2:4). This remark can have no meaning unless one understands John to teach by it that Jesus was aware
of a divine plan overshadowing His actions. Again in chapter
seven, at a later period in His ministry, Jesus refuses the invitation of His brothers to attend the Feast of Tabernacles in Jerusalem noting that "my time has not yet (fully) come" (7:6, 8).
In this instance the time indicated is certainly the moment of His
death. Finally, in 12:23 and 13:1, on the eve of His crucifixion,
Jesus is said to have been fully aware that the long awaited hour
had arrived. In 12:23 the first complete recognition of the hour
is associated significantly with the inquiry of the Greeks concerning Jesus through the disciples, in which the evangelist implies
that the hour of Christ's death is coincident with the origin of the
mission to the Gentiles.

These two themes—Jesus' awareness of His Sonship and His
intuitive knowledge of His work and destiny—come together with
a third theme, the ability of Jesus to bear witness concerning
Himself, in a passage which should be decisive for anyone at-
tempting to determine the evangelist's teaching on this subject.
The verses in question occur in chapter eight, and the teaching
itself is explicitly affirmed in a capsule version in verse fourteen.
In this verse Jesus states His ability to bear witness about Himself in the face of Jewish objections, adding at once that His
ability is based upon a superior knowledge of Himself which
involves an intuitive knowledge of His origins and final destiny.
This is to claim a full knowledge of His person explained in terms
of His pre-existence as the Son of the Father and of His divinely
ordained ministry focused on the cross and the subsequent resurrection and return to heaven (cf. 16:28 and 13:3). According
to this chapter Jesus' witness is unlike that of men. His knowledge may not be understood, as Bultmann tends to understand
it, in terms of an existential possibility presented to all men. It
must be understood as a distinct and unique possibility which
exists for Christ alone. Jesus knows who He is and what He
has come to earth to do, and only He possesses such knowledge.
Because of this fact Christ's witness must be deemed a self-

authenticating witness, depending upon no human words or finite attestation, but solely upon His own words and actions and upon the words and actions of the Father. That is to say, Christ's witness is inevitably self-authenticating because He alone is intuitively conscious of His calling.

A number of scholars have objected to this interpretation of Christ's witness, because of the apparent contradiction between Christ's statements about bearing witness to Himself in 5:31 and 8:14 ("If I bear witness to myself, my testimony is not true" and "Even if I do bear witness to myself, my testimony is true"). But this contradiction is more apparent than real. The solution to the problem is to be found partly in rabbinical precepts regarding the giving of evidence in criminal trials, and partly in reference to the context of each passage. The solution is decisive for the question of Christ's self-consciousness in John.

The Jewish maxims for the giving of evidence in criminal trials were rigidly observed in the disputations of the rabbinical schools as is indicated both by the rabbinic texts and by the procedures at Christ's trial as recorded in the gospels. Three of these maxims bear on these two verses. The first is that no man can bear witness to himself. On this principle Strack-Billerbeck provide the following rabbinical quotations: "A single person is not believed for his own words alone" (Tractate Rosh haShanah 3:1), "No man is believed concerning himself" (Ketuboth 2:9) and "No man can lay down testimony for himself" (Ketuboth 27b). This is clearly a valid legal maxim in any culture, but it was observed with unusual rigidity in Judaism.

The second principle is that in criminal cases at least two witnesses were necessary for the establishment of any fact, a maxim followed closely in Christ's trial and referred to by Him on several occasions as also by Paul and the author of Hebrews. The scriptural foundations for this principle are found in Numbers 35:30 ("No person shall be put to death on the testimony of one witness"), Deuteronomy 17:6 ("On the evidence of two witnesses or of three witnesses he that is to die shall be put to death; a person shall not be put to death on the evidence of one witness") and Deuteronomy 19:15 (". . . only on the evidence of two witnesses, or of three witnesses, shall a charge be sustained"). Strack-Billerbeck note that the first passage is taken by the Midrasch Siphre to provide the principle of double witness according to which other less explicit passages are to be interpreted; that is, every mention of the word "witness" in Scripture must be taken to imply this double witness unless only one witness explicitly is mentioned. As an example of the literal spirit in which this text was taken, the same authors cite an additional passage from the Tractate Pesachim 113b in which God is said to hate, along with false witnesses and those who withhold information when they ought to testify, one who has observed something blameworthy in another but who renders testimony to it without having the verification of a second witness.

The third principle relates to the character of a witness and expresses itself largely as a listing of those who for their personalities, professions or questionable actions were unqualified to render testimony. In this list are found thieves, shepherds (because they seem to have let their cattle graze on other people's land), violent persons, and all suspected of dishonesty in financial matters among whom are tax-collectors and customs officers. In addition Moore notes a passage from the Pesachim 49b according to which the people of the land (the *'am hā'āres*) were not allowed to render testimony. And a passage in the Damascus document from the Dead Sea Scrolls mentions moral character and good standing in the community as prerequisites to witness bearing (10:1-3). In many cases witnesses were adjured to give true testimony in the name of God.

The bearing of these maxims on the texts in question is obvious and in the case of the former entirely explanatory. In chapter five Christ is speaking with the leaders in Jerusalem, the Jews as John designates them (verse 18), and employs an argument *ad hominem* with those who themselves operate on rabbinical principles. It is as obvious logically that Christ's words about Himself *could* be true as it is that He was free at any time to bear witness to His messianic claims. If nevertheless in this case the testimony was inadmissible, it can only be that the discourse is moving within a legalistic sphere.

In 8:14 Jesus intentionally departs from habitual rabbinic procedure. Here the particle with the subjunctive and the emphatically placed first person pronoun give the sense, "But even though I do bear witness concerning myself . . ." and call attention to the special case of Jesus whose self-witness transcends the boundaries of Jewish jurisprudence. Here there is a point of contact, both in the logic and in the psychology of the argument, to the principle of character in witnesses. The rabbis rejected the testimony of men considered unreliable as witnesses; they accepted the testimony of an upright man when substantiated by that of another valid witness. Why then should they not in Jesus' case accept the testimony of one who is greater than men? Christ knows His origin and His destiny, His past and His future, which no other man can know (verse 14); He judges according to truth and not after the flesh as His opponents (verses 15 and 16a); and He works in complete spiritual unity with God the Father (verse 16b). The witness of such a man should be believed on its own merits.

This understanding of the passage is also required if one accepts Hoskyns' observation of a rabbinic-like argument from the lesser to the greater in verse 17, a Kal we-Chomer ("light and heavy") which is Hillel's first rule of exegesis. According to Hoskyns the substitution of the phrase "the witness of two men" for the requirement "at the mouth of two witnesses" which occurs in the original text of Deuteronomy 19:15 is made to emphasize the superiority of the testimony of Jesus. "If we receive the testimony of men, the testimony of God is greater" (I John 5:9).[7]

If these texts are to be interpreted in this manner, as they must be, then they are entirely decisive on the subjects of Jesus' messianic consciousness and witness bearing. Jesus bears a true and perfect witness because He is intuitively conscious both of His origins and of His calling. Only the Son of God can reveal the Father fully. And Jesus is confident of the validity of His revelation simply because He is confident of that fundamental relationship to God.

THE CURRENT DEBATE

It must be acknowledged, of course, that the messianic self-consciousness of Jesus has received such extensive criticism in New Testament studies and has been so criticized that the explicit statements of the gospels, especially those of the Fourth Gospel, are no longer acceptable to scholars for determining in actual fact Christ's own conception of His life and ministry. Today it is one thing to show, as has been done above, that John teaches the full self-consciousness of Jesus. It is quite another thing to affirm that this self-consciousness was characteristic of the historical Jesus Himself.

The most radical contemporary denial of the messianic consciousness is to be found in the Bultmannian camp. These scholars contend, in adopting the methods of form criticism, that the gospels express, not history, but the faith of the early Christian Church and that in consequence little or nothing may be affirmed with certainty about the historical Jesus Himself. In theory this position should rest content with a radical skepticism of all affirmations regarding the messianic consciousness. In actual practice, however, such radical detachment has proved unsatisfactory both academically and religiously; and the old historical studies of Jesus of Nazareth have been followed, in spite of the methodology of the Bultmannian school, and even within it, by the so-called "new quest" of the historical Jesus.

It is interesting in the light of this renewed line of study that even Bultmann, although proceeding in another direction entirely, is unable to rest content with a purely agnostic position and feels compelled to deny categorically, quite beyond the limits of his critical methodology, that Jesus did have a messianic consciousness.[8] It would seem that this view has arisen not so much from Bultmann's interaction with the texts as from his obligation to defend an existential interpretation of Christian faith in which belief rests upon the perception of the meaning of Jesus rather than upon His actual religious and soteriological claims. In this untenable extension of His premises Bultmann's position demands a faith in one who did not understand Himself and calls for a commitment to a position which scholarship itself has increasingly found unsatisfactory.

A clear alternative to the extreme denial of Bultmann and to the radical skepticism of his method has not been lacking in New Testament studies, however. A very different path was suggested by Vos in a work entitled *The Self-Disclosure of Jesus* prior to the second World War. And this line of argument has been furthered more recently by Cullmann in *Salvation in History* which appeared first in German in 1965. These scholars point, as do others even of the post-Bultmannian school, to certain aspects of the Synoptic tradition which in their opinion must be traced to the historical Jesus and which at the same time point to His awareness—one must say His supernatural awareness—of standing in a special relationship to God.

First, Jesus is represented as possessing a consciousness of being able to forgive sins. Cullmann has presented this aspect of the tradition most clearly and has defended it as a radically new and, therefore, authentic element of Jesus' ministry. From this near historical certainty one may argue for the authenticity of all sayings which speak of Christ's victory over sin and the power of the devil.

> Along with all these arguments, the fact that Jesus *forgave sins,* seldom disputed and hardly disputable, seems to me to prove that all the present statements about the victory over Satan have their roots in this self-consciousness. How monstrous Jesus' action must have been in Jewish eyes is something which we do not ordinarily realize. It is not as if Jesus merely proclaimed that the sins of those addressed by him were forgiven; he actually forgave their sins by his own authority. . . . The latter implies a unique consciousness of "being sent" which is more than that of a "herald," and is expressed particularly in Jesus' other statements about himself relating to the *ebed Yahweh* and the Son of Man.[9]

The second aspect of the Synoptic tradition which calls for special notice is the supreme authority exercised by Jesus in His actions and in His teachings. Jesus' ability to forgive sins is an evidence of this authority, but the exhibition of it to which the Synoptics give most attention is the authoritative character of His public teaching. On numerous occasions Christ's authority rivals that of Moses and is understood to do so by the rulers of the Jews. It is interesting to note that both Bornkamm and Kaesemann accept Jesus' claim to authority as a valid historical datum; although Kaesemann, in spite of his desire to join Christ's claim to authority to what he regards as the equally certain fact that Jesus considered His utterances inspired, nevertheless terms the messianic consciousness something which there can be "no possible grounds" for affirming.[10] Bornkamm, although he recognizes a movement of messianic hopes during Jesus' lifetime, nevertheless denies that Jesus Himself claimed messianic titles.[11] At the very least, however, Christ's awareness of His own authority indicates that He placed Himself upon a higher plane than Moses, and to be one greater than Moses was certainly not in Christ's time to be less than the Messiah. It may be argued from this point that Christ's awareness of His authority is dependent, not only upon His ability to proclaim a new and superior Gospel, but also upon His belief that the Gospel was clearly and fully present in His person.

This line of thought leads quite naturally into a third element

of Christ's life and teachings by which Cullmann and others defend the messianic consciousness; namely, the assurance that in
His person the kingdom of God had come. This strand of the
tradition is well expressed in the question asked by John the Baptist in Matthew 11:3 and in Christ's answer to the question: "Are
you he who is to come, or shall we look for another?" Jesus replies to this query by pointing to His works as a fulfillment of the
messianic prophecies in Isaiah 35:5, 6 and 61:1, 2. Thus, the
coming kingdom is identified with that which Jesus Himself revealed on earth through His miracles and the preaching of the
Word. It also falls within Christ's understanding of the coming
of the kingdom in His person that He is often represented as
consciously submitting to a divinely ordained plan of life, as in
the "time" and "hour" passages in the Fourth Gospel.

Taken together these characteristics of the Synoptic narrative
provide a firm historical basis for asserting, in opposition to the
Bultmannian position, that Jesus was aware of being the divinely
appointed Messiah and did in fact ascribe messianic titles to Himself. Cullmann's conclusion that "the early Church believed in
Christ's messiahship only because it believed that Jesus believed
Himself to be the Messiah" is historically sound.[12]

What has been written about the problem of the messianic
consciousness of Jesus in relation to the Synoptics by Vos and
Cullmann does not provide a final answer to all of the questions
associated with Christ's self-awareness, nor does it relate directly
to the subject as it is presented by the fourth evangelist. But it is
not irrelevant to the subject of Christ's witness. The surprising
thing is that in the themes by which the fourth evangelist asserts
Jesus' assurance of being commissioned by God to reveal His
name to men there are also elements, perhaps major ones, which
are strikingly similar to those themes from the Synoptics by which
the messianic consciousness has been thoughtfully affirmed by
conservative scholars. Jesus does not speak much in John about
the Kingdom of God, it is true, nor does He make a point of
forgiving sins. But He does speak with exceptional authority,
basing His claims upon the special relationship in which He as
the only Son stands to God the Father. Jesus also demonstrates
a special knowledge of the divine plan in His history which extends even to an awareness of the meaning and the moment of
His death and to an anticipation of the events which followed it.

In his presentation of Jesus as the divine revealer John does not move within the realm of a myth of revelation. He develops his conceptions upon the firm foundations of historical reality and turns faith not to a hollow center but to One who was and knew Himself to be God's Son and, in rendering His witness, the bearer of a special revelation.

THE CONTENT OF THE REVELATION

In light of the fact that John represents Jesus as the One who reveals the Father and who speaks on earth out of His knowledge of heavenly things, it is an astonishing fact that in the gospel of John with few exceptions Jesus' discourses never contain anything which may accurately be termed a specific or concrete statement about the nature of the Father or of what Jesus has literally seen with Him in heaven. Jesus speaks of what He has seen and heard with the Father, but characteristically John records no information that Jesus actually reveals about God. Jesus is the supreme revealer. But what is the object of the revelation? Does this lack of direct propositional statement about God and heaven mean that Bultmann is exactly to the point when he speaks, as he often does, not of the "what" of the Christian revelation but merely of the "that"? Does it mean that John speaks of a revelation that does not need a content and of a witness that does not need an object?

To be sure, there is a sense in which Jesus does present some limited information about heaven and about the Father. In the farewell discourses just before the crucifixion Jesus comforts the disciples on the subject of His departure by describing a heaven full of rooms prepared for those who love Him (14:2). Jesus speaks of angels descending from heaven (1:51) and teaches that the nature of God is spirit (4:24) and that the Father is the fountainhead of life (5:26). More significant is the fact that Jesus reveals the nature of the Father to be characterized by love. Bernard Weiss develops this aspect of the revelation of Jesus in his *Biblical Theology of the New Testament* and finds the content of the revelation in this characteristic. "But the specific contents of the new revelation of God in Christ is comprehended in this, that God is love." [13] It is noteworthy, however, that of all the texts directly attributable to Jesus and cited by Weiss in proof of this summation—Weiss passes over 3:16 as the words of the evangelist—only one actually makes love a characteristic of God Himself, and that one occurs, not in the public or private teaching of

Jesus, but in Jesus' direct address to the Father in the priestly prayer of John 17 (verse 23).

Again, in a small work entitled *The Revelation of the Father* Westcott speaks perceptively about the title "Father" as a revelation of the character of God. Westcott maintains that this appellation was indeed a new revelation of the relationship of God to men disclosed by Jesus, and for the most part more recent New Testament scholarship supports him—Jeremias, Strack-Billerbeck and others. Since the word "Father" as a form of divine address may be paralleled only poorly in ancient secular and rabbinic texts, it must be acknowledged that in such a sense and in such instances there is indeed something which approaches a content to the revelation about God brought by Jesus.

But the aspects of the content of the revelation mentioned here fall into two classes which are not of equal importance. Many of the things mentioned—that God is spirit, that He has life in Himself, that there are angels in heaven and places prepared to receive believers—are at the best peripheral to the revelation. They are not without importance. But if these are to be called the object of Christ's witness, it is questionable whether the witness is worthy of the means which John has taken to emphasize it. It is not a saving revelation. It is only information. On the other hand, that God may be spoken of as a Father whose nature is to love His children is certainly central if not the essence of what Jesus intended to reveal, especially when these truths are associated, as they must be, with the themes of Christ's death and resurrection. But the striking thing here, and one which is difficult to overlook, is that both of these attributes, the love and the fatherhood of God, are such that they are only known in Christ and in such a way that Jesus can only bear witness to these aspects of the divine nature by bearing witness to Himself. The knowledge of God as the Father really involves the knowledge of Jesus as the Son. And the love of God is seen, not in the academic perception of a rational attribute, but in the life and ministry of Jesus of Nazareth who loved men to the point of dying for them and for their sin.

What is true of the love and the fatherhood of God is also true of everything else that is really known of God. If God is known as truth, it is because Christ Himself is the truth (14:6). If God is known as the executor of saving acts, it is because Christ Himself does the acts which He sees the Father do (5:19).

Jesus' testimony to the Father and to what He has seen and heard in heaven means, therefore, of necessity a self-testimony, a witness to who He is, to Himself. This is the most important thing to be said about the content of the witness of Jesus. It is not simply the revelation of God, but it is the revelation of God in the person of His Son that captures the imagination of the evangelist. Hence, John supplies the content of Christ's witness, not by propositional statements about God the Father, but by the self-disclosure of the Son.

This understanding of the revelation receives further verification from several motifs which are characteristic of the gospel. The first, which has already been suggested, is that Jesus always acts from a position which is subordinate to that of the Father. He is never presented as an independent authority but always as one who speaks and acts in complete accord with the will and the purposes of God (3:11; 7:16, 17; 10:37, 38). Nor is this a partial or temporary dependence. As Bultmann correctly observes, "Jesus' words are not *from time to time* inspired, but he speaks and acts *constantly* from within his one-ness with God." [14] Jesus teaches what the Father teaches, and as a result the Father is seen in all that Jesus says and does. It is a characteristic of the Fourth Gospel that this subordination of Jesus to the Father is maintained alongside of and in complete accord with their highest unity.

A second motif which directs attention to the historical Jesus as the locus of all true revelation of the transcendent God is the Johannine teaching about the "glory" revealed in Jesus. This theme originates in the prologue with the historical claim on the part of the evangelist and disciples that "we have beheld his glory" (1:14) and is developed through the signs ("This, the first of his signs, Jesus did at Cana in Galilee, and manifested his glory," 2:11) to a culmination in Christ's priestly prayer in John 17 in which the glory of the Father is sought through Christ's exaltation on the cross. There can be little doubt that these statements derive their meaning from the visible manifestation of God in the Old Testament through the *Shekinah* and that their purpose for the evangelist is to speak of the visible manifestation of God in Jesus.

That Christ Himself is the object of the revelation is also indicated by all those passages in the gospel which speak of "receiving" Christ or the testimony of the Father concerning Him as that act which secures salvation for the one believing. In the prologue, for example, John contrasts the failure of the Jews to receive Jesus with the saving faith of those who did. "But to all who received him, who believed in his name, he gave power to become children of God" (1:12). And again in chapter five Jesus declares: "I have come in my Father's name, and you do not receive me; if another comes in his own name, him you will receive" (verse 43). The same idea occurs in the first epistle where it is coupled with the idea of testimony: "If we receive the testimony of men, the testimony of God is greater; for this is the testimony of God that he has borne witness to his Son. He who believes in the Son of God has the testimony in himself. He who does not believe God, has made him a liar, because he has not believed in the testimony that God has borne to his Son" (I John 5:9, 10). As Christ Himself is the object of saving faith, so is He also the object of the revelation, a revelation which is in the nature of the case a saving revelation, and of the witness which He makes known to men.

Thus, Christ's witness to the Father, which is at the same time a revelation of the Father, is in reality a witness to His own person and that in such a way that the glory, the words, and the acts of God are to be seen in His glory, His words, and His acts. The successive unfolding of the revelation of God in the Fourth Gospel is coincident with the progressive self-disclosure of Jesus. Jesus bears witness to the Father by bearing witness to Himself. He is the content of the testimony. And this means that Jesus is not only the revealer of the Father. He is Himself the revelation.

This understanding of the content of the revelation receives further clarification when it is developed in contrast to Bultmann's contention that it has no specific content at all. It has been said that Jesus Himself is the object of the revelation, but this statement could presumably be interpreted to mean, as Bultmann understands the sayings of the gospel, that the revelation is only the fact of Jesus' coming. It is true that the primary content of the revelation is not to be found in propositional statements about the Father, and this is the starting point for Bultmann's observations. But Bultmann goes on to say that according to John not only is there no content to Christ's revelation of the Father, in the sense of specific information about the person of the Father, but neither is there specific content to Christ's revelation of Himself. This is to say that Christ's words have no revelational content at all. "Jesus' words communicate no definable content at all except that they are words of life, words of God. That is, they are words of life, words of God, not because of their content, but because of *whose* words they are." [15]

Unfortunately, Bultmann's evaluation does not adequately account for the very thing which is the subject of the present study; namely, the Johannine emphasis upon the words of Jesus and in particular upon the witness of Jesus to Himself in the development of the gospel narrative. It would certainly be peculiar if John, who above all of the gospel writers has dwelt upon the words of Jesus, even to the point of presenting them in elaborate and thematic discourses, wished to stress by such an emphasis, not the content or aspects of the content of the Christian revelation, but only the "that" of Christ's appearance. And it is stranger still, if that be the case, that in the Johannine discourses one finds reference not only to the fact that Jesus has come, but also to the meaning of His coming and to the significance of His actions in so far as these are a revelation of His person. John does not permit his readers to overlook the words of Jesus in his emphasis upon Him as the revealer. Jesus indeed bears witness to the Father by bearing witness to Himself, but He does also bear witness to Himself. This witness involves a content. And this is to say that John's interest in the revelation involves more than the mere fact of Christ's appearance. At the very least Christ's revelation involves the spoken word, and the spoken witness must therefore be considered at least to this extent a content of the revelation.

This does not mean certainly that one must assert *merely* a verbal revelation as the object of Christ's witness. A witness by actions is involved as well. The true object of the witness, as has been said, is Jesus Himself, and this means a Jesus who acts as well as one who speaks. This concentration of the witness in a person must be taken seriously, therefore, not in such a way as to exclude either the words or the actions of the revealer. The claim of the evangelist is that Jesus is the revelation in His totality—not only the fact of His coming, not only what He says, not only what He does, but Jesus as a total person speaking and acting in history. And this means that because Jesus is Himself the revelation, the revelation must involve both His words and actions. These must be united within His person and thus also within the flow of history.

This understanding of revelation, involving a personal unity of word and act, is not a theory which is imposed upon the texts, for it is precisely this personal unity of word and act in Christ that John develops in the gospel. In commenting upon 15:22-24 Westcott calls attention to this unity in pointing out a remarkable parallelism between a declaration about the words of Jesus and a declaration about His works. Westcott arranges the text as follows:

> If I had not come and *spoken* to them, they had not had sin:
> But now they have no excuse for their sin.
> He that hateth me hateth my Father also.
>
> If I had not done among them the *works* which none other did,
> they had not had sin:
> But now they have both seen and hated both me and my Father.

Here the revelation by words and the revelation by works belong together, for they are identical in regard to their source and their ultimate effects. Similarly, in 14:10 the two ideas appear as interchangeable concepts—"The *words* that I say to you I do not speak on my own authority; but the Father who dwells in me does his *works*." This usage indicates that Jesus is the revealer of God in both of these aspects.

Moreover, in the structure of the gospel the words of Jesus are placed in the closest possible connection with the deeds which He performed. The discourse upon the bread from heaven follows immediately and in historical sequence upon the feeding of the five thousand. The judgment upon the spiritual blindness of the rulers of the Jews is uttered with reference to the restoration of physical (and spiritual) sight to the man who was born blind. The identification of Jesus as the resurrection and the life occurs in the narrative of the raising of Lazarus. In these and in other instances the events which are narrated receive an interpretation of their spiritual significance through the discourses. Noting this fact in connection with chapters two through twelve, which he calls the "Book of Signs," Dodd comments correctly that "act and word are one" and that "this unity of act and word is fundamental to the Johannine philosophy, and distinguishes it from the abstract intellectualism or mysticism of much of the thought of the time." [16] The words are incomplete without the acts. The acts are incomplete without the words. And either would be unintelligible without the other.

Finally, it is directly relevant to this argument that John presents the revelation of Jesus as a testimony and, hence, not as proclamation alone nor as the working of mighty acts alone, but as an activity by which both propositional revelation and a revelation by deeds may be combined.

There are many examples of a deed witness in ancient literature, just as of a witness which is manifest by words. Cicero, when dealing with the paradox between the evil in the world and the alleged goodness of the supreme being, can speak of the easy life of thieves as a "contra deos testimonium" (*De natura deorum,* III, 83), and Seneca is able to praise Demetrius by observing, "Non praeceptor veri, sed testis est" (*Epistulae morales,* XX, 9). In each case the life itself is the evidence of the truth of certain propositions.

The best developed conception of a deed witness from Greek literature is to be found in Epictetus. In Stoic philosophy emphasis falls pre-eminently upon the life; that is, upon the moral conduct and the emotional self-control of the educated man, and as a result the true philosopher is the one who can live as well as teach the Stoic doctrines. He is a witness by his life as well as by his words. On this basis and much beyond its deserts the peripatetic and uncompromising life of the Cynic receives great praise from Epictetus (*Discourses,* III, xxii), and the moral discipline of Socrates is repeatedly brought forward as an example of a perfect way of life. In one discourse a witness by deeds is even cited in apparent dismissal of logical argument in order to impress the student with the need for philosophic conduct: "What is lacking now is not quibbles (*logaria*); nay, the books of the Stoics are full of quibbles. What, then, is the thing lacking now? The man to make use of them, the man to bear witness to the arguments by his acts. This is the character I would have you assume, that we may no longer use old examples in the school, but may have some examples from our own time also" (I, xxix, 56, 57, Loeb translation). The implication is that the words without the deeds are of little value and that the true philosopher must be a witness by his acts. In some circumstances, as in that of Socrates, it is understood that a deed witness could mean the acceptance of death for the sake of a persuasion.

From the conception of a deed witness in Greek literature it is possible to move directly to the witness of the martyrs as that witness is finally defined in the writings of the fathers. When

Tertullian (*Ad martyres,* 1) and Cyprian (*Epistula,* 10) are at pains to distinguish between a martyr and a confessor on the basis of the former having suffered death for his confession and the latter having been released from custody even though he had been able to render an identical testimony, it is evident that the conception of a witness by deed, in this case by death, is uppermost in the distinction. There can be no doubt, of course, that this technical use of *martys* in the fathers is a later one, brought about on the crest of the *lapsis* controversy by the growing influence of the confessors in the church. But the definition adopted at this point is certainly connected with pre-existing connotations of the terms, and it is probable that this connection is sufficient cause to explain the technical restriction of the word *martys* to one who had died for the sake of Jesus Christ. The application of a witness by deeds to Christian martyrs was certainly underway by the time of Clement, who speaks of Peter as one who "endured not one or two, but numerous trials, and so bore a martyr's witness and went to the glorious place that he deserved" (I Clement 5:4). The complete martyr terminology is already present in the Letter of the Churches at Lyon and Vienne to those in Asia Minor (A.D. 177-178).

It would be a mistake, however, to think that by the discovery of a deed witness in the martyr or philosopher one had found an adequate parallel to the union of word and deed witness which is characteristic of the Johannine portrait of Jesus Christ. In Greek as also in Latin literature the deed witness is striking and important, but it is no more than an illustration of doctrine or a proof of its validity. Word and deed witness do not really exhibit an organic relationship, and the life and the doctrine are each comprehensible without the other.

In the Old Testament there is a far more unseverable connection. It has been noticed more than once and in more than one connection that in biblical thinking word and act are characteristically united, especially in so far as this observation applies to the self-revelation of God. This unity is fundamental to the Old Testament interpretation of historical development. The connection is crucial for an understanding of the exodus and the conquest of Canaan, for instance, for the revelation at Sinai and the divine instructions for the battles are inseparable aspects of the events. The same may be said for the revelation given through the prophets. Here word and deed are often equally important aspects of the message, as for instance in the symbolic acts of Jeremiah (chapters 13, 19, 27 and 32), Ezekiel (chapters 4, 5, 37:15-28) and Hosea, and even the prophetic word itself is frequently looked upon as something done as opposed to something only said. In the Old Testament the word of God is always word and deed, and one cannot be exaggerated at the expense of the other.

At the same time it must be said that the relationship between word and deed in the Old Testament is not as organic nor as vital to the revelation as is the case with Jesus Christ. In the Old Testament word and deed are more than parallels. They interpret one another, and they are united within the flow of history. But as Brunner notes, "No event in the history of Israel is *the* act of God, no prophetic word is *the* word of God. No fact becomes the decisive revelation of God, and no word, as such, is the fact of salvation." [17] By the focusing of revelation in Jesus Christ, the witness by deeds and the witness by words receive a unity in the New Testament and especially in John which is unmatched in the Jewish Scriptures. It is the unity of a personality. And this is true both of Christ's own witness in the world and also of the Father's witness in the Son, both of which are, of course, expressions of the same reality. In Christ God's testimony is complete. In Him God has spoken His final word and has performed His definitive action. As Barth correctly observes, "The New Testament tradition has set forth the revealing activity of Jesus as an intertexture, impossible to dissolve, of word and deed, and indeed of word and miracle." [18]

"I AM . . . THE TRUTH"

Further light is shed upon the nature of Christ's witness by the prominence given to the idea of *truth* in the Fourth Gospel, for Jesus is said to bear witness not only to the Father and to Himself but also to the truth. John the Baptist had a special role in pointing to the truth (5:33), but in a profoundly deeper sense this was the object of Jesus' incarnation and earthly ministry. "For this I was born, and for this I have come into the world, to bear witness to the truth" (18:37). Against the background of this purpose it is not surprising that the adjective is used to characterize Christ's testimony ("My testimony is true," 8:14) and that the same attribute identifies the Holy Spirit who is to carry on His work (14:17; 15:26; 16:13; cf. I John 4:6; 5:7).

The basis for this distinctive and stimulating usage of the conception of the truth in John lies in the fact that in Greek as also in Hebrew the words for truth may denote the essential nature of God or of divine reality as that which is "genuine" or "trustworthy" as opposed to all which is illusory or variable. The root meaning of the Hebrew word *'eměth* is that which is "firm" and therefore "solid," "valid," or "binding." As a religious term it denotes a reality which belongs to God's essential nature, is the foundation of all God's acts and words, and which is and must be the essential characteristic of the religious man (Psalms 15:1, 2; 51:6). Thus, in general the Hebrew conception of truth is active and leads not so much to wisdom as to moral integrity and obedience to the Mosaic law. When John speaks of doing the truth in 3:21, it is evident that the thought is in sympathy with the Hebrew connotations of the term.

The Greek word *alētheia* denotes "truth" as opposed to falsehood, rather than "trustworthiness." Yet, because it finds a context within Greek philosophy as well as within the legal sphere, the word also denotes that which is ultimately "true" or ultimately "real" as, for instance, God or the Platonic world of ideas in distinction from the world of visible phenomena. It is significant that on the basis of this usage John is able to employ the Greek word for truth in a manner not fundamentally different from the religious usage of *'eměth* to denote the essence of the divine nature (cf. 7:28 and 17:3).

Therefore, when John says that the testimony of Jesus is true or when Jesus speaks to define the purpose of His coming as a mission to bear witness to the truth, the thought is greater than the idea of merely speaking the truth. Jesus' words are true, of course, but John does not mean only this. Even less does he mean that Jesus' spoken words are the summation of all that which is true. Jesus had many things to say which the disciples were incapable of receiving (16:12), and in Christ's own speech the Holy Spirit is cited as the One who will later lead the disciples into all the truth concerning Him (16:13). What John means is that Jesus' words partake of the nature of the divine reality and that speaking the truth when applied to the ministry of Jesus really means the revelation of the divine reality to men. Thus, John writes that "grace and truth came through Jesus Christ" (1:17). And Jesus says to the Jews, "Now you seek to kill me, a man who has told you the truth which I heard from God" (8:40).

His words are uttered to make known a new fullness of truth, and this new fullness of truth is to be conceived as a revelation from God, and of God, who alone is true and trustworthy. At 8:44-46 the contrast between the divine and anti-divine reality is emphasized by a distinction between the lies of the devil and the truthfulness of God; and in 8:14, when Jesus describes His testimony as "true," the statement immediately assumes the further suggestion that His testimony is revelation (cf. also 8:40).

In several cases a man's being of the truth is made a prerequisite of receiving the divine revelation (4:23, 24; 18:37; cf. 3:21), and in 8:32 truth is portrayed as that which is able to make men free when once it is received. This means, as has already been intimated, that the truth proclaimed by Jesus as revelation is a saving truth and that consequently the revelation itself is a saving revelation. In 5:24 the idea of a saving revelation is further expressed by the claim that "he who hears my word and believes him who sent me, has eternal life; he does not come into judgment, but has passed from death to life."

John also says that not only are certain individuals of the truth and not only is the testimony of Jesus true, but Jesus Himself is the truth and that, not only in a partial or a metaphorical, but in an absolute and literal sense. John teaches that "grace and truth" came through Jesus Christ (1:14, 17). And Jesus says, "I am the way, and the truth, and the life" (14:6) as also, in reference to Himself: "He who seeks the glory of him who sent him is true, and in him there is no falsehood" (7:18). In no instance is the meaning simply that the words which Jesus utters are true or merely that they embody the reality of God, both of which are, of course, correct, but rather that He Himself is the perfect embodiment of that divine reality which His life in its fullest extent revealed to men. He is truth because the Father is completely present in His person.

All that is to be found of God and of spiritual reality by men is to be found in Christ and in the scriptural and prophetic revelation which points to Him. Jesus brings life to men because He is Himself the life of men (1:4; 14:6). Jesus brings light (1:5, 7) because He is the light (1:9; 8:12), just as He brings down bread from heaven because He is the bread from heaven (6:25-59). In the same way He makes known and imparts the truth because He is Himself in His essential nature determined by the truth. Jesus is Himself the revelation; Christ is the object of His witness.

A true and saving knowledge of the Father will be gained by men only by a true and living knowledge of the Son.

One other fact must not be overlooked, although it does not receive much consideration in many commentaries. In chapter seventeen the Old Testament is introduced as that which also embodies the truth in a way which does not and cannot conflict with the incarnation of the divine reality in Christ.

Jesus prays in verse 17 that the disciples might be sanctified "in the truth," noting at once that "thy word is truth." And again in verse 19 He prays that they might be sanctified "in truth." Does "thy word" refer to Christ Himself along the lines of the Logos idea in the first and fourteenth verses of the prologue? This is unlikely in view of the strong assertions throughout the prayer that Jesus has been faithful in delivering the words of God to the disciples (verses 6, 8, 14) and that the disciples are in their turn to proclaim this word to others (verse 20). At the very least Jesus is speaking of His teaching. Thus, the word of 17:17 must be identified with the words spoken by Jesus about Himself in this world on the basis of what He has known concerning His relationship to the Father, and the claim that the words are truth must mean that the divine reality is also embodied in these words as revelation.

It is hard to doubt, moreover, that the "word" mentioned here also has reference to the Old Testament Scriptures, for the idea of a sanctification by the word refers in Jewish idiom to the development of an internal righteousness by a reading and a study of the Torah. In the first place, the reference is literally in the singular—"thy word," not "my words"—and is identified by means of the pronoun with God. Moreover, in his analysis of this text Westcott finds the same phrase used by Jesus to occur also in a Jewish prayer for the New Year and to occur in such a way that the "word" is clearly identified with Scripture—"Purify our hearts to serve Thee in truth. Thou, O God, art Truth, and Thy word is Truth and standest for ever."[19] Strack-Billerbeck cites a number of similar prayers for sanctification through the commandments of God. A third argument arises from the probability that in speaking of the "word" as truth Jesus is to be understood as quoting from Psalm 119:142, which certainly has reference to the law of Moses. And the variant reading ("thy word is truth") is even closer to the verse in John. To use "truth" to define this "word," as Jesus does here, would, therefore, mean that the divine reality which is disclosed in Jesus and in His speech to men is no other than that divine reality which had been revealed to Israel in the Mosaic Scriptures and that the divine reality revealed in Jesus is such that it may be, and in fact has been, revealed in written words as well as in a person. To the early Church, which relied heavily upon the Old Testament Scriptures in the explanation of Christ's person and in the defense of the meaning of His coming, the written and the living word belonged together.

That Jesus bears witness to the Father by bearing witness to Himself, both by word and deed, and manifests the truth to men by being Himself the truth, points to a unity of the modes of revelation which can only be called *organic* as opposed to any view of revelation which centers the object of the revelation in a limited aspect of Christ's existence. Three such inadequate views have come to light. The first is that of Bultmann who would perceive the real revelation only in the fact of Jesus' coming. There is no literal content to the revelation at all according to this understanding. Equally inadequate are the attempts to teach that revelation centers only in the events of Jesus' ministry or, from an exclusively rationalistic approach to Christianity, that the revelation consists solely in the religious propositions to be found in Jesus' teaching. It is not only words or only acts any more than it is only the bare fact of revelation which is the object of Christ's witness. John teaches, upon the basis of his understanding of the witness of Jesus to Himself, to the Father and to the truth, that the words and acts belong together in the unity of the person of the revealer. He Himself is the revelation in all that He says and does, and the Old Testament Scriptures as a partial and previous revelation point to Him.

CHRIST THE LOGOS

An organic understanding of the Christian revelation is repeated again in a new light and with additional implications in the Johannine doctrine of the Logos. Christ has appeared on earth as God's witness, and John has emphasized accordingly both the specific words (plural) of Jesus and the idea of *the* Word (singular) by which he introduces Jesus in the opening verses of the gospel. Jesus is the Logos who speaks the words of God. He is the Word upon whom all other words are centered. In the expression of these ideas the conception of the Logos and the significance of Christ's words parallel the theme of Jesus' witness and explain to a large degree why in John's sight there can be no conflict between the varying types of witness, the modes of the divine revelation, particularly between the scriptural revelation of the Old Testament era and the personal revelation of the new era centered in Jesus Christ.

There are a number of ways in which the Greek noun for "word" is used in the Fourth Gospel, and these form an indispensable background to a proper understanding of the Logos.

1. There is a common usage by which *logos* denotes the spoken word, uttered by one man and heard by another. In these instances the term is approximately synonymous with *rhēma* ("that which is said," "a word") and *lalia* ("speech," "speaking"). Thus, when the woman of Samaria reports to her friends the things which Jesus has said to her, there are many who believe in Christ "on account of the word (*logos*) of the woman" (4:39) and others who believe not for her words but for the word (*logos*) of Jesus (4:41, 42).

2. In addition to the common use of *logos* to denote the spoken word, there is also a theological or religious usage which is almost inevitably present whenever the gospel speaks of the words of Jesus. Jesus' words take on a depth of meaning and abiding character which is impossible to the words of men. As healing words they impart health (4:50). As saving words they impart life (5:24). As divine pronouncements they possess the same authority and validity as Scripture (2:22; 18:9, 32). Christ's words, like Scripture, will never pass away, and these will be present at the last day to execute judgment on those who reject them. "He who rejects me and does not receive my sayings has a judge; the *word* that I have spoken will be his judge at the last day" (12:48).

3. *Logos* is also used to denote the sum total of Jesus' teachings. In this sense Christ's *logos* clearly denotes the Gospel, the *kerygma,* which is to be proclaimed by the Church in imitation of Christ (17:20) and is to be believed and obeyed by those who hear it (8:31; 14:23, 24; cf. Rev. 3:8). Jesus' word is to be received into the heart (I John 1:10; 2:14) because it is able to cleanse the heart (15:3) and to impart eternal life (5:24; 8:51, 52).

This use of the word is linked to the theme of revelation, by reference to its source and by John's understanding of the truth. When Jesus is before Pilate He declares that He has come into the world to bear witness to the truth (18:37), thereby associating His words with revelation. And in conversations with the Jews He repeatedly describes His message by this characteristic (8:32, 40, 45, 46).[20] Dodd concludes: "Along with other quite ordinary uses of the term, the Fourth Evangelist uses the term *logos* in a special sense, to denote the eternal truth (*alētheia*) revealed to men by God — this truth as expressed in words (*rhēmata*), whether they be the words of Scripture or, more especially, the words of Christ." [21]

4. The fourth and most striking use of the word *logos* is the application of it to Christ Himself. He is the final and perfect word of God to men. With this idea the evangelist presents Jesus Christ not only as the perfect revealer of the Father and as the perfect revelation, ideas which have already been presented through other concepts, but he does so in such a way that Jesus' ability to bear a perfect witness depends, not upon His earthly circumstances nor ultimately upon His spiritual perception, but upon who He is in His essential nature. Christ speaks the words of God because He is the Word.

The gospel contains four instances of this usage, and all are in the prologue (1:1-18)—three times in the first verse and once in verse fourteen:

> In the beginning was the Word, and the Word was with God, and the Word was God.

> And the Word became flesh and dwelt among us, full of grace and truth.

In addition Jesus appears in much the same light in two of the other traditional Johannine books although not termed simply the Logos as in John. In I John 1:1, in an introduction to the epistle which inevitably recalls the prologue to the gospel, Jesus is called the "Word of life," and in Revelation 19:13 he is called the "Word of God." These two references occur in contexts which do not appreciably amplify upon the ideas in the prologue; consequently, it is to the prologue and to the use of the term in non-biblical texts that one must turn for an understanding of the Logos Christology.

In the prologue to the gospel of John, the evangelist develops a twofold identification of Jesus: as the pre-existent Son of God, and as the mediator of creation and revelation. The first part of the prologue (verses 1-5) is concerned in general with Christ's ontology, His being. This section, separated from the second by a parenthetical and contrasting reference to John the Baptist in verses 6-9, presents Jesus as the divine hypostasis who existed with God throughout eternity and who was active in the creation of the world. Within this section verses three through five form a unit of their own. For with verse three the tense shifts from the continuous, timeless imperfect to the aorist, and the activity of the Logos is introduced in connection with a description of His being. Here, as also later (verses 10, 12), although ostensibly dealing with His ontology, John is already thinking functionally in defining the Logos by His actions. It is the nature of the Logos to be active, and these verses presuppose John's ruling conception in the following chapters that Jesus is the sent one, the divine messenger of God. The second and third sections of the prologue (verses 9-14 and 16-18), also separated by a reference to the Baptist in verse 15, are concerned specifically with the meaning of Jesus' ministry, especially His revelational activity, and present Him as the historical focal point of all divine saving revelation, the unique source of life and light, of spiritual rebirth and spiritual illumination.

This twofold identification of Christ—by His ontology and by His activity—is the same identification of Jesus implied in John's use of the Logos formula. In reference to the prevailing Greek conceptions, John's Logos would recall the qualities of pre-existence and divinity as well as Christ's function as the mediator of creation. To the Jew steeped in the Old Testament Scriptures, the Word would recall the activity of God in creation and in revelation. Thus, in introducing the Logos idea into the prologue, John avails himself of an idea which is basically compatible with what he seeks to teach, and expresses by this concept and by explicit statement his understanding that Jesus of Nazareth is the one who existed with God from the beginning and was God and who had appeared on earth for the saving revelation of the Father (see Appendix). John's use of the Logos idea is, therefore, in perfect accord with the emphasis, previously noted, upon His witness as revelation.

It is of the greatest significance to observe also that these two aspects of the identification of Jesus are not unrelated, for it is precisely because of who Jesus is that He is able to effect a definitive and saving revelation. This truth can hardly be overemphasized. Jesus is not to be considered an emanation of the divine as in the revelational hierarchies of the Gnostic world nor, as in Docetic thought, as one on whom the divine spirit came. Jesus is Himself the Logos who existed with God from the beginning, and He is Himself divine. It is significant to this facet of the Logos Christology that the word itself, although of little frequency even in the prologue, occurs at exactly the two places in the introduction in which the pre-existence of the Logos and His passing over into history are most explicitly described (verses 1 and 14). Jesus is able to witness to the Father, in the sense of a definitive revelation of the Father, because He is Himself the pre-existent Logos, the creative and revealing word of God. Jesus reveals God because He is God. He speaks the words of God because He speaks as God. Barrett perceives this truth in his discussion of the prologue by terming Jesus "an ontological mediator between God and man," which is to say, "a mediator of true knowledge and of salvation," and Hoskyns adds that "from the beginning, and throughout his work, he [John] makes it clear that the words of Jesus are meaningless apart from their relation to the word of God, that the apostles are insignificant apart from their relation to the man Jesus, and that Jesus Himself profiteth nothing unless He be the incarnate Word of God." [22] In the doctrine of the Logos John provides an answer to the question of how it is possible for Jesus to be the revealer of the Father and at the same time lifts the understanding of Christ's witness to the highest understanding of His person. It is because Jesus is the Logos that John can make the claims for Him that he makes throughout the gospel.

As interpreted in the light of the prologue and of the use of the word throughout the gospel, however, the Logos idea also does more than relate the ministry of Jesus to His divine nature and pre-existent activity. In a number of areas it also introduces a fusion of ideas which serve to heighten the significance of Jesus and of His testimony.

First, by referring his introductory comments about Jesus to the Logos, John has also indicated that the revelation which has come in Jesus is not to be separated from the revelation which had gone before in the era of the Old Testament and in the Old Testament Scriptures. This fact has already been noted in commenting upon the meaning of "truth" in John 17 and elsewhere. Jesus is not a new revelation if new is taken to mean that which corrects or is radically different from that which has gone before. Rather in Jesus is to be found the full expression of that revelation of God shining in the world at all times, embodied specifically in the Scriptures, and now in the last days manifest in human flesh. It is significant that *Logos* is also used of the Old Testament Scriptures in the phrases "the word of God" or "his word" (5:38; 8:55; 10:35; cf. also 12:38). In this perception John is not far from the opening verses of the epistle to the Hebrews in which the revelation of God through His Son is intimately connected with the speaking of God in Old Testament times through the prophets and in which, significantly enough, attention is also given as in John to the activity of the Son in the creation of the world and to the revelation of God in Christ in terms of God's *speaking* to men through Jesus. Jesus Christ is entirely in the stream of the divine revelation in history. And Jesus is in this stream and not outside of it or in opposition to it simply because He is the same one who has been active and, indeed, the only one who has been active in the revelation of God at all times in the past. The unity of all such revelation is thus to be found in Jesus who is at once its source and object.

At the same time it must be said by way of anticipation of the discussion of the apostolic witness and the witness of the Holy Spirit that the significance for revelation of the title Logos does not lie entirely in the past and present; that is, solely in the scriptural revelation of the Old Testament and in the earthly ministry of Christ Himself. That Jesus is the pre-existent and eternal Logos is also significant for all future revelation. Thus, according to the fourth evangelist, the same Jesus who was active before His incarnation preparing for it through the revelation given in the Old Testament is also active subsequent to the period of His incarnation, providing a definitive interpretation of the events of that period through the normative witness of the apostles and applying the truths of His ministry to those who believe through the divinely guided preaching of the Gospel and the continuing sacramental ministry of the Church. This post-incarnate ministry is also a function of the Logos and is carried forward through the Holy Spirit which is imparted to believers subsequent to Christ's return to heaven. There is every reason to think that, more than any other aspect of Christ's revelation, it is this present ministry of the exalted Logos in the Church which most holds John's attention and which finds the most consistent emphasis in the language and the structure of the gospel.

Moreover, just as the themes of the prologue and the doctrine of the Logos suggest a fusion of various aspects of revelation in Jesus, so also does the relationship between the Logos Christology and the emphasis throughout the gospel upon the words of Christ suggest a fusion of propositional and personal revelation in Him. It is possible *a priori,* of course, that the conception of the Logos and the emphasis upon the *logoi* have no connection at all, that John has merely adopted a current philosophical term without feeling at all obliged to relate it to the other uses of the same word throughout the gospel. But this is not the case with the fourth evangelist, nor would one expect it to be, considering John's careful and creative attention to his terms. The words of Jesus play such an important part in the gospel that it is difficult to imagine that John did not also think of these words in his identification of Jesus as the Logos. And the fact that the narrative uses the same term to denote the Gospel of salvation makes a connection in thought quite probable. Jesus speaks the words of God, Jesus makes known the Gospel, and He does this precisely because He is Himself the Word, the Logos. The designation of Jesus as the Word and the emphasis upon His words belong together.

Now, if this connection in thought is to be accepted, it suggests that although the revelation begins and is centered in Jesus, it is focused in Jesus, not as in a thing, but as in a person who reveals Himself by His words and actions. It is a maxim of Old Testament scholarship that the God of Israel is known through His actions and through the scriptural revelation which describes and explains these actions. In the same way, in the Fourth Gospel Jesus is known through His acts (the miracles of healing and His symbolic gestures) and through His explanatory words, upon which, indeed, John has laid the greatest stress. The words and the Word belong together because the Word completely embodies the reality of the teachings and the teachings express the characteristics of the Word. Thus, the revelation is focused in Christ, but it is not proposition*less.* At the very least it is by the propositions as well as by the actions that the person of the Logos is disclosed and by His self-disclosure that God is known. If necessary the words may be called a means of the personal revelation to be found in Christ. But they are means only in the sense that they are themselves a part of the revelation which has its object in Jesus and contribute along with the revelation in the Scriptures, by the prophetic word, and in Christ's signs and wonders to the recognition and acceptance of God Himself as He is offered to men in Him.

Finally, the same connection between the Word and the words suggests that because the Logos is unique, because there is none other than Jesus who perfectly knows and who perfectly reveals the Father, so are the words of Jesus unique. This thought echoes the teaching that Christ's words were unlike the words of the rabbis, who repeated the words of other men or merely cited Scripture. Jesus' words were His own in the sense that they were the words which He alone had heard in the presence of His Father. There is no substitute for the revelation embodied in Christ's witness.

In all of these themes the Johannine use of the *logos* terminology is in perfect harmony with and even amplifies what has earlier been described as an organic revelation involving, at the same time and in the closest possible unity and inter-dependence, a personal, a verbal, an active, and a scriptural communication. All of these terms are concerned with revelation. And their organic unity is found where alone it could be found — in Jesus Christ who has been active as the Logos in all revelation in the past and who in His incarnate form unites a verbal and an active witness in Himself. Jesus is the self-communication of God. Where Jesus speaks God speaks. Where Jesus acts God acts. And Jesus has been speaking and acting from the beginning, as the evangelist indicates in the opening verses of the prologue. What comes to expression in the flow of history in the person of Jesus of Nazareth is only that which existed in the nature of God from before creation. It is John's achievement that he is able to present Jesus as the unique bearer of the divine revelation through the use of the Logos terminology (both the Logos and the *logoi*) and that he does so in such a way that the person of the historical Jesus becomes the organic focal point of all divine disclosure. Godet has expressed this aspect of John's intention in the prologue admirably. "In applying to Jesus the name Word, John . . . wished to describe Jesus Christ as the *absolute revelation* of God to the world, to bring back all divine revelations to Him as to their living center, and to proclaim the matchless grandeur of His appearance in the midst of humanity." [23]

THE WITNESS OF JESUS CHRIST

In the preceding sections of the present chapter the discussion of the witness of Jesus Christ has generally followed the lines set by the Johannine material, from the more basic and less complex ideas to those themes which are less pervasive and more complex. Thus, the study has considered in sequence: Christ's being sent from God, His messianic consciousness, the content or object of His witness, and the meaning of the Logos as that term is related to His testimony. In many of these sections, however, the ideas associated with the witness of Jesus overlap, correcting and reinforcing one another. Hence, it may be helpful to provide a more systematic and logical statement of the teaching of the Fourth Gospel on the subjects of Christ's witness and revelation by way of summary. The truths which have been uncovered in the previous sections may be grouped as follows:

1. Jesus Himself is the object of His witness, the content of His revelation. This does not mean that the revelation fails in being a true revelation of the Father, a conclusion which would be often contradicted in a reading of the gospel, but that the revelation of God recorded in the gospel is a personal revelation provided in the person of His Son.

2. Christ's ability to communicate this revelation, to bear witness to the Father, is founded upon who He is. Jesus is the Logos. He is at once both God and man and so communicates the Father to man in and through the disclosure of Himself.

3. The revelation so provided may not be restricted to one particular aspect of Christ's earthly life or ministry, whether to the fact of His coming, to His mighty acts, or to His spoken words. The revelation is centered in Christ in His totality, which means as a total personality speaking and acting within history. Thus, the revelation is to be found in all of Christ's words and in all of Christ's actions.

4. As the personal revelation of God to men Jesus makes known in His own person the essential character of the Father described by the attribute of truth. By such a description and by the application of the same attribute to the Old Testament Scriptures the evangelist indicates that the revelation which is expressed in Jesus' words and acts, while above all else a new and full revelation of the Father, is nonetheless of one reality and in true continuity with the revelation made known to Israel

before His incarnation. As the Logos it was Jesus Himself who was active in this preparatory revelation. And as the Logos He continues to be active—in the normative, human witness of the apostles and in the responsive, missionary witness of the Church through the ever expanding proclamation of the Gospel.

5. In all of these forms several things characterize the Christian revelation. First, the revelation communicated in Christ and embodied in the Scriptures is by its very nature a *mediated* revelation. It provides no direct vision of the Father, but creates the human possibility of recognizing the Father as He is revealed in Jesus. Second, because of Jesus' superior knowledge of God and of the relationship of the Father to Himself, the revelation of Jesus is ultimately, although reinforced by many compelling evidences, a *self-authenticating* revelation. And third, this revelation is at the same time a *saving* revelation, for it has as its object, not a direct theophany or a mystical experience, but the opportunity for a man to experience salvation. He is to know the truth, for the truth will make him free (8:32; cf. 20:30, 31).

Chapter 4

The Divine Testimony to Jesus Christ

THE WITNESS OF THE FATHER

In the fifth chapter of the gospel of John, in conversation with the Jews, Jesus appeals to a number of supplementary witnesses in defense of His extraordinary claims (5:31-47). Jesus had declared Himself equal with God and the bearer of God's saving revelation. He had claimed to be the giver of life and the One who is entrusted with the judgment. Upon what evidence are these claims based? Why should the Jews believe such testimony? In answer to these questions and in deference to the procedures of Jewish law, Jesus cites three independent testimonies which reinforce and corroborate his own.

First, there is the witness of the Baptist (verses 33-35). The Jews had acknowledged the significance of this testimony when they sent to John to hear his message, and John had identified Jesus as the Christ. The Jews should accept this testimony. Moreover, there is another witness which is greater than the witness of the Baptist. Jesus also has the witness of His signs (verse 36). The miracles are greater than John's testimony because they are the direct witness of God the Father in whom and through whose power the miracles are performed. Finally, there is the witness of Scripture (verses 37-40). Since it is this divine revelation upon which the Jews most clearly base their hopes of salvation and to which they pretend an unwavering allegiance, it is in the light of this testimony that the unbelief of Israel is most openly revealed for what it is. Thus, the last witness is explicitly connected with the judgment.

In appealing to the witness of the Baptist, the signs, and the Scripture, Jesus is producing evidence for the testimony which

He had already given to Himself. And this means, if the appeal to such evidence is to be taken at all seriously, that with the shift from Christ's own witness to the supplementary witnesses of chapter five, the focus of the present study must also shift from the theme of the direct, supernatural revelation in Christ to the problems of the authentication of His religious claims. This does not mean that the idea of witness is no longer concerned with revelation; for, as will become evident, the authenticating witnesses to revelation are themselves revelation. Nor does it mean that the revelation so described ceases to contain the personal element which was prominent in the case of Jesus Christ. There are personal characteristics in the objectifying elements as well, and their whole purpose is to elicit a personal response to Christ in faith. What it does mean is that next to the words of Jesus, in which His claim to be the revealer is expressed, there must also be placed the threefold witness of chapter five which corresponds with and bears witness to the truth of His teaching. Each of these witnesses must be viewed in the total context of the gospel.

It must also be said by way of introduction that Christ's appeal to such evidence should be taken for what it is and should not be dismissed beforehand on the basis of any preconception regarding the nature of revelation or of its verifiable or non-verifiable characteristics. In particular it must not be assumed categorically that revelation is non-verifiable, for then the objective value of such evidence is lost, even though other aspects of the evidence may be retained. Neither may the importance of the witnesses be disregarded by arguing *a priori* that revelation cannot bear witness to revelation, as if an appeal to such evidence were merely circular reasoning. The nature of the authentication of revelation is quite different from that which is implied in this objection, and God must be allowed to testify of God. Finally, it must not be assumed without careful attention to the evidence itself that revelation cannot be given in a plurality of forms. All of these objections contain elements of truth and considered in their place deepen one's understanding of the revelation. But assumed categorically beforehand they render a true appreciation of the Johannine evidences impossible. The witnesses to be considered in this chapter are preparatory for belief and are promises of the full revelation which is manifest in Christ. They possess an importance which is secondary to the witness of Christ's words. But they are not dispensable. They are themselves revelation, although of a limited and preparatory kind. And they are not at all opposed to the personal revelation which has been made known in Christ.

In appealing to such external and supplementary evidence Jesus is not just appealing to facts or circumstances. In appealing to the witness of the Baptist, signs, and Scripture, Jesus is really drawing attention to the witness of the Father which is made on His behalf. Just as He is content to seek the will of God in all His acts and sayings, so is Jesus content to let God bear witness to His claims (5:30, 31). That is why these witnesses are revelation. And that is why they are important. It is, therefore, correct to view this chapter as the *divine* testimony *to* Jesus Christ, and thereby to set it off from the divine testimony which is borne by Jesus to Himself, from the human witness which is borne on His behalf, and from the divine testimony in the heart of the believer which is the witness of the Holy Spirit. It is significant that this section of the gospel begins with a reference to the Father and to the inherent reliability of His testimony: "If I bear witness to myself, my testimony is not true; there is another who bears witness to me, and I know that the testimony which he bears to me is true" (5:31, 32).

A number of readers may object to this reference on the basis of the work of several commentators on the Fourth Gospel and many of the Fathers, arguing that the "other" of verse 32 is actually John the Baptist. But everything in the context serves to refute this contention. In the first place, the witness of this verse is referred to by means of a present participle ("the one testifying") and the present tense ("the testimony which he is testifying"). The second witness, the witness of the Baptist, is referred to in the past ("he bore witness"). This contrast is made all the more striking by the fact that the witness of the Baptist is sometimes given a present significance elsewhere (cf. 1:15 and the present participles in 5:35). In addition, the full form of the expression—literally, "the testimony which he is testifying"—has the effect of setting the first testimony apart for special notice, and this concern for a special and corroborative witness accords well with other Johannine references to the Father's testimony (8:18; I John 5:9; cf. Heb. 2:4 and I Cor. 2:1). The question posed by verse 32 is, therefore, not so much the identity of the "other"—the "other" is the Father—but, granted the reference to the Father, in what does His supreme testimony consist? How does the Father bear His witness? What specific evidence or evidences are indicated by this appeal?

Chrysostom spoke of the witness of the Father as the voice from heaven which was given at the baptism, and in this he has been partially followed by others.[1] This view is supported by the fact that the idea of a voice from heaven, a *bat kol* (a daughter of the voice; i.e., an echo of God's voice), was an important phenomenon in Judaism and is of relatively frequent occurrence even in the New Testament. By this heavenly sign God was presumed to bear direct evidence to a man, to a doctrine, or to a point of dispute. Thus, the Tosefta Soṭah notes that "when the last prophets, Haggai, Zechariah, and Malachi, died, the Holy Spirit ceased out of Israel; but nevertheless it was granted them to hear [communications from God] by means of a mysterious voice" (13:2). In later Judaism the importance of this sign declines, however, perhaps to some degree as a reaction to the revelational claims of Christianity, so that some time after A.D. 70 there is a case of Rabbi Joshua ignoring a voice from heaven on the grounds that the Torah is not in heaven, and later a rule is even formulated requiring a rabbi to reject the evidence of miracles (such as a *bat kol*) when deciding halakic questions.[2] In spite of the reference to such a voice in chapter twelve of the gospel, however, it is evident that John does not call attention to this phenomenon as a witness, and there is no reason to read either this or a similar incident into the context of chapter five.

A number of scholars perceive a direct witness of the Father to the Son through the internal witness of the Holy Spirit and believe that this is the witness indicated, just as an indirect witness is later indicated through the signs and Scriptures. It is enough to observe in this connection that although the witness of the Spirit is certainly a divine witness and is an important phenomenon in John, nevertheless the witness of the Spirit is not really introduced until the final discourses and then only as something which is to be experienced subsequent to Christ's death and resurrection.

The first suggestion actually based upon the text of chapter five and actually proceeding upon exegetical grounds follows from the observation that if the "other" of verse 32 is to be taken as the Father, then this verse must be considered in connection with verses 37 through 39 in which the witness of the Father is also mentioned and is perceived to be given in the Scriptures. It might be thought that the references to God's voice and to God's form in verse 37 are actually references to a *bat ḳol* and to a theophany in which the revelation of the Father and His witness are seen to be conveyed. But this conclusion is misleading. In actual fact this passage alludes to the revelation of God at Sinai, and at Sinai, in spite of the thunder and the clouds, the people themselves did not hear God nor did they see His form. What they did receive was Scripture. Thus, in denying the witness of the Scriptures to Jesus the people actually prove that, although they are Jews by birth, they have no part in the revelation given to Israel in the wilderness, nor in the true Israel who accepts and believes the promises which were received there.[3]

If this procedure is the right one—arguing from the reference to the Father in verse 37—then it is also difficult to doubt that the witness of the Father is intended, too, in verse 36 in which Jesus alludes to the works "which the Father has granted me to accomplish." It must be remembered in this connection that Jesus claims to do only what the Father Himself does (5:19; 10:37, 38) and affirms that the Father is working in His actions (14: 10). The works include more than the miracles. They include all of Jesus' actions, the miraculous as well as the non-miraculous, and in them the Father testifies directly to the Son. It is interesting to note that no less weighty and diverse commentators than Calvin, Godet and Bultmann join the signs to the Scriptures in this manner in speaking of the direct witness of the Father to Christ's claims.[4]

If the witness of the Father may have a plurality of forms, the question immediately arises as to whether John may not also conceive of the witness in other ways, in chapter five and elsewhere. An excellent indication that he does so is found in the major text on witness in the first epistle (I John 5:6-12). In this context the testimony of God, which is greater than the testimony of men (verse 9), is indicated as being at least the internal witness of the Spirit and the witness of the water and the blood (verses 6-8). Thus, whatever the exact implications of the witness of the water and of the blood, it is evident that John considers the testimony of the Father to be pluriform. This does not mean, of course, that all of the forms of witness are indicated or implied in the references to the Father's testimony in the fifth chapter of the gospel, for it has already been observed that there is no cause to think of a voice from heaven or of the witness of the Spirit in this connection. What it does mean is that the way lies open to recognize the Father's witness in whatever other evidence John marshals in the discourse.

The other witness to which Jesus alludes is John the Baptist. Can it be that John's testimony also falls within the category of the Father's witness? It is true, of course, that John's is the witness of a man, as opposed to the witness of the signs and Scripture, and that Jesus therefore speaks of a witness which is greater than that of John. But it must not be forgotten that the Baptist is twice spoken of as a messenger who has been sent by God to Israel (1:6; 3:28) and that John appears in Israel as a prophet and, hence, as one who speaks the words which were spoken to him by God. For this reason it appears proper also to think of John's witness as a divine authentication and to speak of chapter five as the formal presentation of the witness of the Father to the Son, involving in progressive sequence the witness of the Baptist, the witness of the signs, and the witness of the Scriptures. These three represent the evidence of the prophetic word, the acted word, and the written word. And in every case one must perceive the word of God. The value of such testimony is to be traced precisely to the fact that it is the testimony of the Father.

THE WITNESS OF JOHN THE BAPTIST

Nowhere in the Fourth Gospel is the preoccupation of the evangelist with the subject of witness more prominent than in the case of John the Baptist and nowhere does the permanent validity of supplementary evidence for the claims of Jesus Christ receive a greater clarity of expression than in the evangelist's treatment of John the Baptist's testimony.

In John the ministry of the Baptist is transformed, as over against the appearances of the Baptist in the Synoptics; and it is transformed in such a way that the witness of John emerges as the supreme prophetic witness to the claims of Christ, a witness complete in itself and permanent in its effects. The evangelist does not modify the content of John's witness to the themes of the gospel, nor does he adapt John's claims about Jesus to the claims of Christ Himself. In the Fourth Gospel the witness of the Baptist stands alone. It is monolithic. And it is appealed to as a whole on four occasions: in the prologue (verses 6-8 and

15), in the formal presentation of the Baptist's testimony together with its effects upon the first disciples (1:19-51), in the supplementary testimony of John at Aenon near Salim (3:22-30), and in the final appeal to the Baptist's testimony by Jesus in the citation of supplementary witnesses in chapter five (verses 33-35).

The most noticeable feature of the Johannine version of the ministry of the forerunner and one which has been repeatedly noticed in the commentaries is the absence from John's account of many traits most characteristic of all the earlier narratives. For example, John omits all reference to the ministry of the Baptist as a preacher of repentance and all mention of him as the herald of the imminent kingdom of God. The Baptist does not issue a call to repentance in the Fourth Gospel, nor does he actually engage in baptism, although the allusions to a water baptism in 1:26 and 3:22-26 indicate that the evangelist presupposes a knowledge of this ministry on the part of his readers. When John meets the priests and Levites in Matthew's gospel, he denounces their hypocrisy, terming them a "brood of vipers" and pointing to his own baptism as a way of repentance and of salvation from the wrath to come (Matt. 3:7-10). In the Fourth Gospel, by contrast, a similar encounter appears in an official character without apparent conflict and is the occasion for the formal presentation of the Baptist's testimony (1:19-34).

Even more significant than these alterations and omissions is the fact that the evangelist neglects to report the baptism of Jesus Himself, an event which is the crowning point of John's ministry in the Synoptics. Apparently the actual baptism has little interest for the evangelist, for it has little theological meaning in itself. Instead everything has been focused in Christ. Instead of the baptism there is Jesus. Instead of an act there is a verbal proclamation. In the light of these facts it is hard to doubt that the evangelist's procedure involves a transformation of interest through a process of selection, governed, as Dodd believes, by John's "avowed purpose to exhibit the Baptist as the great witness to Christ." [5]

While the account of John's ministry is lacking in many of the traits characteristic of the Synoptic gospels, it is no less striking that it is also lacking in themes peculiar to the Fourth Gospel. This fact points to the same observations reached above, but it contains the added suggestion that the evangelist desires to preserve John's testimony accurately and without alteration. It is particularly noteworthy in this connection that although the evangelist has indicated in the prologue that the Baptist was sent to bear witness to the light, the actual testimony of John presented later does not contain a reference to the light, nor does it bear an allusion to His glory. John does not identify Jesus as the vine, the shepherd, the bread from heaven or the water of life.

Moreover, just as John's words do not develop the themes of the gospel, neither does the gospel develop the themes which are present in the Baptist's witness. If this were the evangelist's intention, the obvious starting point would have been the Baptist's designation of Jesus as "the Lamb of God, who takes away the sin of the world" (1:29). And yet, despite the implications of the evangelist's apparent ordering of the passion narrative so that the crucifixion of Jesus takes place at the moment when the paschal lambs are being sacrificed, the theme of the sin-bearing lamb does not recur. From such circumstances and others one must infer that John looked upon the stories concerning the Baptist, not as a tradition to be molded to his predominantly theological interests, but as a storehouse of material from which he has attempted to extract solely the Baptist's explicit testimony to Jesus.

The evidence for this conclusion is not merely negative. It has already been noted in passing that for the actual baptizing of Jesus the evangelist has substituted the spoken identification of Jesus as the Messiah, thereby focusing the reader's attention upon a verbal testimony rather than upon an external act. The same shift is evident in other matters as well. It must be observed especially that even where the evangelist has included incidents in his account which are narrated in the earlier gospels, as for instance the voice from heaven at the baptism and the descent of the dove as the visible sign of the presence of the Spirit, these incidents are included not as objective events occurring simultaneously with the narration, but as past events which find a place only as aspects of the Baptist's verbal testimony. As Loisy justly observes, "Everything in the dialogue is arranged in such a way as to place value upon the testimony of the forerunner, and, as if the flow of the conversation were not sufficient, he [the evangelist] explicitly praises the perspicuity of his discourse."[6]

It is another and most conclusive proof of this distinctive Johannine interest that the words for witness replace "preaching"

(Matt. 3:1; Mark 1:4; Luke 3:3) and "exhortation" (Luke 3: 18), which the Synoptic writers use of the Baptist's ministry, and that John's terms (*martyrein* and *martyria*) occur as early as the prologue where they direct all attention toward the Baptist's witness. In John's evaluation the Baptist emerges as the witness *par excellence,* and John indicates his interest in him precisely as a witness and in his testimony as the first, great and definitive identification of the person and the ministry of the Lord. Nowhere else in the gospel is there such a one-sided preoccupation.

John's severe selection of his material does not mean for an instant, however, that John has not been meticulous and even elaborate in the actual ordering of the material which he preserves. Just as the evangelist has limited his witness terminology to terms *martyria* and *martyrein* while at the same time developing the application of these ideas far beyond the remainder of the New Testament books, so has he limited his interest in the Baptist to the single theme of the forerunner's testimony while at the same time developing that one theme far beyond its previous implications.

The outline which John has developed for presenting his material concerning John the Baptist is stated quite clearly in the prologue and has been identified with much clarity by Dodd in an exhaustive treatment of the Baptist material in John.[7] It has three parts. John writes that the Baptist, who was sent from God: 1) was not the Light, but 2) was sent to bear witness to the Light, in order that 3) all men might believe through him (verses 6-8). This, as Dodd indicates, is precisely the outline which the evangelist follows in the verses immediately following the prologue.

The elaborate section which is introduced by the statement "and this is the testimony of John" (1:19), the equivalent of a section heading in a contemporary publication, and which is concluded by another significant emphasis upon the witness borne by John in verse 34, is divided into two nearly equal units which correspond precisely to the first two points of the foregoing schema. John is not himself the Light. He is not the Messiah (verse 20); he is not Elijah (verse 21a); and he is not the prophet (verse 21b). He is only a voice crying in the wilderness, the voice prophesied by Isaiah in 40:3. In observing that John identifies himself by this passage, it might be thought that the

evangelist is intending to improve on the Synoptics, in which
Isaiah 40:3 appears as editorial comment upon John's ministry
(Matt. 3:3; Mark 1:2; Luke 3:4) and not on the lips of John
himself. But the text is quoted with current relevance in the Dead
Sea Scrolls (Manual of Discipline, 8), and it is by no means
improbable that John may have himself described his preaching
in this light.

In the second place, John does bear witness *to* the Light (verses
29-34). In a formal declaration which goes far beyond the Synoptics he expressly identifies Jesus as the sin-bearing lamb, as
the one who baptizes with the Holy Spirit, and as the pre-existent
Son of God. This makes the Baptist the pre-eminent witness to
the incarnation.

The final section of the three part schema is filled out in verses
35-51, in which, as a direct and also an indirect result of the
Baptist's testimony, the first believers are led to follow Jesus.
These are the first two disciples (Andrew and an unnamed fol-
lower) and, as a result of their testimony, Peter, Philip, and
Nathanael. The two-part development of the Baptist's witness
in 1:19-34 has been clearly noted by many commentators, but
in the light of John's explicit statement in the prologue it is certainly right to carry the formal presentation of the Baptist's witness as far as its effects in the concluding verses of the chapter.

The evangelist's marked attention to the results of John's testimony is of the highest significance in the light of Christ's appeal
to John's testimony in chapter five (verses 33-35). John's testimony was given in order that men might believe. And so they
did. This was the object of his witness. It is interesting to note
that the text cited by Dodd as providing the schema for the Baptist material in John (1:6-8) sets forth the belief of men as the
ultimate object of the Baptist's witness in just this fashion, em-
ploying a succession of relative clauses in a characteristic Greek
construction. John came for witness *in order that* (as a specific
object) he might identify the Light and *in order that* (as a final
object) all men might believe. The witness of the Baptist was
the first and great testimony to Jesus, and as such it was perfectly
adequate to lead a man to faith. The lack of faith manifest on
the part of the unbelieving Jews must be traced, therefore, not
to a deficiency in the evidence for Christ's claims, as some commentators imply, but to causes quite beyond the evidence, namely, to the blindness of the Jewish rulers to the truth of the Chris-

tian revelation. In this respect as in others the citation of John's testimony in chapter five presupposes a knowledge of the events of chapter one.

It must be added to the preceding analysis that the Baptist does not appear only as the first and great witness to Jesus Christ. He also appears as a particular type of witness. And that type of witness is the *prophet*. It might be assumed from his rejection of any claim to be identified with the Messiah, with Elijah or with *"the* prophet," that John the Baptist also rejects the prophetic role itself, but such a conclusion would betray a misreading of the evidence. What John denies in these rejections is a claim to importance on his own. He is not *the* prophet of Deuteronomy 18:15. But that does not mean that he rejects a prophetic function. In fact it is precisely in pointing away from himself and solely to the Messiah that he emerges most strongly in this role.

It is noteworthy in the first place that as a priest and Nazarite John was the perfect figure of the prophet. This point is not emphasized by the evangelist, but there can be no doubt that he presupposes this understanding of the Baptist's mission, just as he presupposes a knowledge of John's ministry of baptism. It is against the background of the common recognition of the Baptist as a prophet, for example, that one must understand the questions of the Jewish deputation (1:19-28). The prophetic character of John's mission is also specifically recognized by the twice repeated assertion that John came, not on his own accord, but as one who had been sent by God. This note is struck first in the prologue—"There was a man sent from God, whose name was John" (1:6). And it is asserted a second time by the Baptist himself in chapter three—"I am not the Christ, but I have been sent before him" (3:28). The latter statement has its origin in the words of Malachi ("Behold, I send my messenger to prepare the way before me," Malachi 3:1) and parallels the use of this particular quotation in Mark 1:2, Matthew 11:10 and Luke 7:27. Thus, even in the Fourth Gospel John the Baptist appears with a divine commission, as have all the prophets.

John the Baptist also *speaks* as a prophet, however, and this is to say, not as a teacher alone nor as an expounder of Scripture alone, but as one who communicates a direct, divine revelation. This revelation is a supernatural occurrence, the supernatural character of which is most clearly indicated by the external sign, the descent of the dove from heaven (1:32-34). It was this revelation, either externally or internally perceived, that enables John to conclude his testimony with the categorical claim: "I have seen and have borne witness that this is the Son of God" (1:34).

There is also a sense in which John's ministry as the prophetic forerunner of the Messiah was constituted by a revelation prior to and in preparation for the sign which was given at the baptism. John's testimony to Jesus hinged upon the reception of the sign, but the real testimony was to the fact of Christ's divinity, defined in terms of sonship, and this testimony presupposes a previous call and a previous communication for its foundation. This message John passes on to his contemporaries. It is true that on several occasions the evangelist has John repeat the confession that "I myself did not know him" (1:31, 33), but this only indicates that the preparatory revelation was a partial one and that it waited upon the sign for its completion. The expectation of the Messiah preceded the witness of John. Thus, John speaks, not as one who proclaims the advent of the Messiah on the basis of his own understanding, but as one who speaks a message which has been directly revealed to him by God. In this respect the Baptist follows in the line of all the Old Testament prophets and bears a witness which is itself the climax of the prophetic revelation.[8]

Although the Baptist bears witness to the full revelation which has come to men in Jesus by sharing in the divine revelation, both in his original call with its directives for his ministry and in the sign received at the baptism of the Lord, this does not mean that he is himself the revelation as is the case with Jesus Christ. Instead, John participates in the revelation, received revelation, in order that he might point away from himself to the One who is the organic focal point of all divine revelation in history. Jesus says that John "was a burning and shining *lamp*" in whose light the Jews were willing temporarily to rejoice (5:35). Here "shining" points, not to a light which shines in its own right, as to a "burning light," but to a lamp which has been kindled from a source outside itself, a "kindled light." John is not the Light. Only Jesus is the Light. But John bears witness to Jesus precisely because he has been kindled by Him.

Jesus teaches the same thing by saying that John "has borne witness to the truth" (5:33), for John bears witness to Jesus through having his own testimony determined by the truth, that divine reality which came to full expression in the Lord. The evangelist repeats Christ's teaching in his own words by terming John only a "voice" as opposed to his designation of Jesus as the pre-existent "Word."

One further characteristic of the supplementary testimony in the Fourth Gospel also comes to expression in this connection, and although it is also true of Scripture and of the signs, it is particularly evident in the case of John the Baptist. John's witness has *a permanent character, an abiding validity*. It is presented as an established datum. And as such it exercises an influence which extends beyond the lifetime of the Baptist. This characteristic of the witness is important, for it is true of the other witnesses also and plays a vital role in the connection between witness and judgment.

The permanent validity of the Baptist's witness is implied throughout in John's treatment of his message. In 1:7 it is said that John bore witness to the light in order that *all* men might believe through him. Although the faith of the first disciples was a partial fulfillment of that purpose there can be no doubt that the evangelist conceived of John's witness as one which must endure, directing not only the disciples, not only all Jews, but all men everywhere to Jesus. This is the motivation behind the evangelist's formal presentation of his witness. It is significant in the same connection that the final message of the Baptist in 3:25-30 is followed, neither by an account of John's imprisonment nor by a narration of his death at the hands of Herod (cf. Matt. 4:12; 11:2-15; 14:1-12; Mark 1:14; 6:14-29; Luke 3:19, 20), but only by Christ's appeal to John's testimony (5:33-35). Once John has spoken his witness is complete. Now, he testifies for the readers of the gospel. The same point of view emerges strikingly in regard to the tenses which the evangelist employs to speak of the Baptist's witness. Even in the prologue, in which the activity of the Baptist is considered in the past—"he came . . . to bear witness to the light" (verses 7, 8)—the witness takes on a formal, timeless quality. And in verse fifteen, especially, the evangelist uses the historic present to observe that, "John bears witness concerning him." The evangelist achieves the same effect by the present participles "burning" and "shining" in 5:35. In these sentences the Baptist's testimony emerges as an established

datum and with a permanence analogous to the abiding validity
of Scripture.

The comparison of the Baptist's testimony with Scripture
should make it evident that the emphasis placed here upon the
effect of the Baptist's testimony does not lose its significance as
a result of the fulfillment. And it would be most correct to say
that it is the fulfillment which gives the preparatory witness its
true and permanent validity.

One cannot forget, moreover, that John is also a figure of the
new just as he is a figure of the old, at least according to the
Fourth Gospel. John is the last of the Old Testament prophets,
but he is also singled out from all other expecting figures as one
who perceives and identifies the One to whom he bears his witness. This observation has led Dodd to speak of the Baptist as
"the first Christian confessor" to the Lord [9] and has led Barth
to write perceptively:

> Apart from his being a contemporary of Jesus, it is not at all
> clear at first sight how far he really belongs to the New Tes-
> tament. According to the Synoptists, at any rate, his function
> is almost wholly Old Testament. . . . But this line of exposi-
> tion is strangely intersected by another. Jesus calls him more
> than a prophet (Matt. 11:9). And according to John 1:20f.,
> not only does he not claim to be the Christ, but not even to
> belong to the independent order of the forerunners of the
> Messiah. . . . The difference between the witnesses before
> and after is very clearly discernible in the person of John, but
> all the same it seems neutralised. . . . The preparedness of
> the prophets becomes in John the thanks of the apostles, so
> that necessarily the thanks of the apostles is recognizable in
> the preparedness of the prophet.[10]

It is interesting in this connection that the witness of the
prophets as preserved in the Old Testament and the witness of
the apostles as preserved in the New Testament both possess that
abiding permanence which is also clearly discernible in the case
of John the Baptist.

THE WITNESS OF CHRIST'S SIGNS

Although John the Baptist speaks as a prophet and with the
authority of a prophet, it is still only as a prophet and hence only
as a man that he appears before the Jews. The witness of John
is valid and binding, but it is verified ultimately only in its fulfill-

ment. Thus, Jesus adds to the evidence of the Baptist the direct
and inescapable witness of his signs. "The testimony which I
have is greater than that of John; for the works which the Father
has granted me to accomplish, these very works which I am
doing, bear me witness that the Father has sent me" (5:36).
What are these works? And how does John conceive of their
witness to the claims of Jesus Christ?

The best answer to these questions begins with the term which
John uses most characteristically in speaking of Christ's miracles.
John calls them "signs" (*sēmeia*). And the connotations of this
term prevail even when the evangelist also speaks as he often
does of Christ's "works" or of his "signs and wonders." All of
these expressions are common throughout the Old and New Testaments, and all quite frequently mean "miracle," an event which
is contrary to the usual course of nature. But *sēmeia* does not
always mean miracle. And in its original associations it denotes
a reality which is quite distinct. It means a "distinguishing mark"
or "token." Thus, in the Old Testament circumcision is termed
a sign or a token of the covenant (Genesis 17:11), and this usage
is repeated precisely by Paul in Romans 4:11. In the same manner finding a baby in a manger becomes a sign to the shepherds
(Luke 2:12), and the "sign of Jonah" becomes a token of Christ's
death and resurrection (Luke 11:29, 30). In Rabbinic Judaism
the word is even taken over directly into Hebrew to indicate a
word or a phrase used as a mnemonic device to suggest a passage
of the Torah.

A "sign" is, therefore, something of a symbol, a pointer to
something signified. It is apparent that a miracle may become
a sign by indicating the presence of a divine personage or of a
prophetic figure who has been authorized by God.

As signs in this sense the miracles in John point to the glory
and the divinity of Jesus. This is made quite evident in the case
of the miracle at Cana where the motive of the transformation,
as John tells it, cannot really be found in a compassion for human suffering or in the conquest of Jesus over evil, the two prevailing motivations in the earlier narratives. The motive is solely
that the glory of the Son might be revealed and that the disciples
might believe as a result of the revelation (2:11). The greatest
miracle of all, the raising of Lazarus from the dead, has as one,
if not its chief motive, the desire that those present might see the
glory of God (11:40). And John concludes his narrative with

the observation that "Jesus did many other signs in the presence
of the disciples, which are not written in this book; but these are
written that you may believe that Jesus is the Christ, the Son of
God, and that believing you may have life in his name" (20:
30, 31). In every instance the sign draws attention to Jesus Himself and consequently to the divine nature which finds a partial
revelation in His works.

There is a sense, too, in which the sign is also something more
than a symbol. The sign can also partake in some measure of
the thing symbolized, so that the reality is communicated along
with the external indication. Here the symbolic acts of the
prophets may be cited as an archetype as, for instance, the symbolic representation of the siege of Jerusalem by Ezekiel with a
piece of tile and an iron plate (Ezek. 4:1-3). Dodd comments
quite correctly in reference to this particular example that "the
prophets appear to have thought of such symbolic acts as more
than mere illustrations. They were inspired by God, and in His
unchanging purpose formed the necessary prelude to that which
He had determined to perform. . . . In the symbol was given also
the thing symbolized." [11] It is certainly not misleading to think
of the Reformed doctrine of the sacraments in this connection,
according to which the reality of the promise is communicated in,
with, and through the partaking of or immersing in the elements.

This higher meaning is particularly dominant in John. Jesus
performs signs, but they are not intended merely to make men
marvel or merely to direct men to Himself. The signs contain
the reality, and the reality which is communicated is, not merely
divine power or divine grace, but Jesus Christ Himself, the Truth,
the glory of the Word of God. This is to say that the signs become vehicles of revelation, but not as channels only. Rather the
signs themselves are a part of the revelation. Christ is revealed
in them. And they are an aspect of Himself. If this is true, it
will be seen at once that this teaching supports what has already
been termed in other language a personal revelation of God in
Jesus, involving both Christ's words and His symbolic actions.
The signs are not mere appendages. They are part of Christ and,
therefore, also of His revelation. It is another aspect of this understanding that some of the signs also take on abiding significance as prototypes of the sacraments and thus also of the continuing presence of Jesus in the Church.

It should also be noticed that all of the references to Christ's "works" in John also come under the principles of interpretation which have been outlined in reference to the signs. Christ's *works* are also signs, not just His miracles. And this means that strictly speaking all of Christ's actions, all of His works, are symbolic in the particular sense which John intends by his understanding of the signs. Both His supernatural acts and also His so-called natural acts fall under the directives of the Father and are acted out in the fullness of his power. All alike are revelational. This is why it is possible to speak of the many works (9:3; 10:25, 32, 37, 38; 14:10, 11; 15:24) as one work which Jesus came to earth to do (4:34; 17:4).

In the nature of the case, however, some of the works of Jesus are more significant than others. Some reveal one aspect of His ministry, some another. Thus, John's own interests compel him to select out of many works at his disposal those which are most instructive for the Church and most central to a true understanding of Christ's person. John chooses suggestive miracles. He frequently speaks of other signs (2:23; 3:2; 6:2, 26; 7:31; 9:16; 20:30), but he feels free to omit many of them, chiefly the miracles of healing and of the casting out of demons which the Synoptic writers have included. He chooses miracles which have consequences in belief or disbelief. And these interests govern him when, in other instances, he includes a miracle which occurs in the Synoptics but inserts it into his gospel in such a way that a deeper meaning is suggested than is the case in the previous narrations.

Among the many works John pays particular attention to the following:

1. *The transformation of the water into wine* (2:1-11). By John's own indication this was the first of Jesus' signs (2:11), and with the entry into this narration the reader passes from the formal presentation of the witness of the Baptist to the formal presentation of the signs. This sign had its immediate object in the manifestation of Christ's glory, as has already been noted, and it resulted in the belief of the disciples. It is hard to doubt that this sign is also meant to demonstrate the unity of the Father and Son in creative power (cf. 1:3) and to indicate Christ's function as the bringer of messianic joy of which the wine is probably a symbol. The transformation may also have reference to the replacement of the Jewish purifications by the sacrament of the Christian eucharist.

2. *The healing of the nobleman's son* (4:46-54). John calls this the second sign which Jesus did after He had come from Judaea to Galilee (4:54), and this sign also results in faith. It is hard to imagine that the nobleman exercised no faith in his appeal to Jesus. But the nobleman's faith is not praised in John as in the similar stories in the Synoptics (Matt. 8:5-13; Luke 7: 1-10), nor does John actually say that he believed until after the working of the sign (4:53). It is a further indication of this single interest that Jesus speaks explicitly of a faith which is provoked by signs and wonders (4:48) and that John alters the miracle from a scene of pure compassion, as in the Synoptics, to a revelation of Christ's power over sickness.

3. *The healing of the impotent man* (5:1-18). The third sign follows immediately upon the healing of the nobleman's son. In this incident Jesus again exhibits a power over sickness and exercises His authority upon one who apparently was weak in faith (5:6, 7) and whose greatest loyalty even after the healing was ostensibly to the Jewish rulers (cf. 5:15). In this healing as in the previous one the life-giving power of the divine word is central to the miracle. On the symbolic level the episode presumably points to the saving power of Christ in Christian baptism or to the replacement of the ineffective Jewish order with its baths and purifications by the spiritual power of the indwelling Christ.

4. *The feeding of the five thousand* (6:1-14). This event is a borrowing from the Synoptic tradition (Mark 6:34-44; pars. Matt. 14:13-21; Luke 9:10-17; cf. Mark 8:1-10; Matt. 15:32-39), and it is the first of the signs which John develops verbally by means of one of Christ's great discourses. The sign is significant in itself as an indication of Christ's power to give (spiritual) life and as an indication of the relationship which a man must have to Him. But it is also an obvious symbol for the Christian eucharist. This theme emerges clearly in the discourse and is also suggested obliquely by the introductory allusion to the Jewish passover, the parallel to the Christian sacrament under the Old Testament dispensation (6:4). This sign makes clearer than the others that the object of the signs is the communication of Jesus Himself to men in faith. Jesus says, "I am the bread of life; he who comes to me shall not hunger, and he who believes in me shall never thirst" (6:35). In reading these words the student of the gospel is to think, not merely of the spiritual communication of Jesus Christ by faith, but of the historical figure

presented in the gospel, the one who brings the revelation, who is Himself the revelation and who is continually presented to believers in the Christian eucharist. The general disbelief of the people is first mentioned in connection with this liturgically oriented narration.

5. *The walking upon the water* (6:16-21). It is not easy to determine whether John intends the walking of Jesus upon the water as a sign or whether he has merely appended it to the account of the feeding of the five thousand on the force of the Synoptic tradition. John does not call attention to the incident. But if it is to be taken as a sign, it obviously indicates Christ's power over the laws of the natural order. John does not say, as he does with the other signs, that this demonstration provoked either faith or disbelief on the part of the observers.

6. *The healing of the man born blind* (9:1-41). The sixth of Jesus' signs embraces a double miracle, involving the restoration of physical and spiritual sight to a man who had been born (spiritually and physically) blind. The two miracles presuppose each other. And the lesser of the two, the physical miracle, is a striking indication of the other. The theme of the narration is the coming of the light into the world, and the revelation is portrayed as light in this narrative just as it is portrayed as life in the story of the feeding of the multitude. By contrasting the faith of the man born blind with the lack of belief on the part of the Jewish authorities, John suggests a judgment beginning in the present against those who, confronted with the light, prefer to live in darkness.

7. *The raising of Lazarus from the dead* (11:1-46). In the last of the public signs Christ's progressive display of power over nature, sin and sickness comes to a climax in the total victory of life over death. In this episode the discourse is mingled with the narrative, the thematic statement of which is Christ's claim to be "the resurrection and the life" (11:25). Dodd observes correctly on the meaning of this miracle: "first, that eternal life may be enjoyed here and now by those who respond to the word of Christ, and, secondly, that the same power which assures eternal life to believers during their earthly existence will, after the death of the body, raise the dead to renewed existence in a world beyond." [12] Dodd also adds as a third point that, because Lazarus will die again and because it is not exactly correct to see him as an example of the Christian resurrection for that reason, it is

right to regard him as a sign himself. For he points beyond himself to Jesus who at the moment of the miracle was upon the point of dying for men and of becoming the firstfruits of the Christian resurrection. It is significant that the raising of Lazarus is specifically appealed to as a sign (12:18; cf. 11:42), for this supreme manifestation of the glory of Jesus leads, not only to belief on the part of the observing multitude, but also to the most extreme denial on the part of the authorities (11:45-53; 12:17-19).

8. *The resurrection of Jesus Christ* (20:1-29). Strictly speaking the resurrection of Jesus Christ does not fall among the other signs. Unlike the previous episodes Christ's resurrection is not described by John, nor is it observed by the world of men at large. Instead Christ appears only to believers and that in the most intimate and revealing circumstances. All this is true, and yet it is impossible to omit this event as a final and conclusive indication of Christ's glory. In 2:18 and 19 Jesus Himself alludes to His coming death and resurrection as a sign, and on two occasions He employs the verb "to signify" in reference to His crucifixion (12:33; 18:32). This sign excels all others in its ability to lead men either to belief or disbelief. It was the chief if not the governing element in the missionary preaching of the early apostles. And since Jesus is most clearly revealed in His death and resurrection, it is the sign to which all of the previous signs are directed. That is, it is only in the light of Christ's personal victory over sin and death that any of the previous signs can be truly understood—from the first changing of the water into wine as a revelation of the new life and messianic joy disclosed in Jesus to the resurrection of Lazarus as a promise of the Christian resurrection.

In the light of this brief survey of the Johannine miracles it can hardly be wrong to conclude that in some cases at least and often to the exclusion of all other motivations the signs have the revelation of the glory of Jesus as their object. The signs themselves are revelation, and Jesus performs them, not primarily for the sake of His compassion for a suffering humanity, as in the Synoptics, but to demonstrate His divine nature and supernatural power and thereby to provoke faith in the observers. On the lowest possible level the signs demonstrate the unity of creative power which exists between the Father and the Son, the same unity which was first suggested in the prologue (1:3). Where

Jesus works God is working. Thus, God Himself is seen in all Christ's works and actions. On a slightly higher level the signs also communicate the reality, in addition to symbolizing or suggesting it. In this sense the revealer and the revealing sign are inseparable. Finally, the signs also suggest the continued presence of Jesus in the Church, and thereby tend in many instances to have a theological if not a directly liturgical bearing upon the early Christian sacraments. This aspect of the Johannine miracles has been developed extensively by such scholars as Dodd and Cullmann.

It is to be observed, too, that in many cases the sign does not occur alone, but is connected with a verbal interpretation. This is particularly true of the later signs—the feeding of the five thousand, the healing of the man born blind and the resurrection of Lazarus—where a discourse accompanies the narration. But it is also implied even where a miracle is not followed by a discourse, for it is hard to escape the conclusion that other signs also require an interpretation on the part of the reader and in fact provoke it. It is significant in this connection that many of the miracles seem to leave off at their highest point without apparent sequel—the changing of the water into wine, the healing of the nobleman's son, the walking upon the water and others — and thereby compel response inevitably. The witness of the signs is such that it is to be taken together and in the closest possible manner with the words. The truth of this statement has led Barth to speak of the Christian witness as concerned exclusively with speech, with words, and has permitted Bultmann to declare, although with all the distortions of the categorical, that "in fact the miracles in John are neither more nor less than words, *verba visibilia*" and that "the works of Jesus . . . are his words." [13] The miracles in John are not isolated events to be considered in themselves but divine events which must be taken together with Christ's divine words and are thus a part, but only a part, of the whole fabric of the divine revelation.

As part of such a revelation it also follows that the signs are opportunities for faith and are not occasioned by it as is the case in the Synoptics. The signs do not presuppose faith. The signs disclose the glory of the Son of God and thus demand it. There is a sense in which the gospel speaks of a faith occasioned by an external sign as an inferior faith (4:48; 10:37, 38; 14:11). But although a faith based solely on the signs is an inferior faith, it is nevertheless a true faith, for it directs the expectations of the believing one to Christ. Thus, John does not hesitate to allow Jesus to point repeatedly to the signs and the wonders He performed. The works reveal His glory and bear witness that the Father has sent Him (5:36). In chapter ten Jesus appeals on three consecutive occasions to their testimony. "The works that I do in my Father's name, they bear witness to me" (10:25). "I have shown you many good works from the Father" (10:32). "If I am not doing the works of my Father, then do not believe me; but if I do them, even though you do not believe me, believe the works, that you may know and understand that the Father is in me and I am in the Father" (10:37, 38).

Finally, the signs are not only symbols which point to a reality, not only bearers of that reality and themselves a part of the entire fabric of the divine revelation. They are also in a poignant sense a *trial,* an occasion for belief or disbelief. They are a temptation in the profound sense in which Deuteronomy employs the term (Deut. 4:34; 7:19; 29:3). Accepted they lead on to life. Rejected they intensify man's sin and lead to judgment. In the signs, as also in the witness of the Baptist and the witness of the Scriptures, the Jewish people and all men have a challenge to belief and the opportunity of discerning Christ's real nature to the consequent salvation of their souls. Disbelief renders them inexcusable. And disbelief is the beginning of the judgment.

Christ's Signs As Evidence

In a number of recent studies, most of them from the hand of German scholars, it has become almost an unchallenged procedure to dismiss the significance of corroborative evidence for the Gospel and to declare instead and as an opposing principle that revelation may only be received by faith. This procedure necessarily involves the witness of the Baptist and that of Scripture. But it is particularly observable in reference to the signs. It is claimed that signs are inadequate to move a man to faith and that the spiritual truths to which they testify are incapable of rational verification. Although the claim itself expresses certain elements of truth, other aspects of this basic assumption run directly counter to the Johannine doctrine of testimony and revelation.

Many illustrations of this posture may be given. Campenhausen states, quite correctly if the matter is considered from only one perspective, "The signs by which the Johannine Christ declares his authority are no proof upon which unbelief may fasten." [14] And Brox adds in much the same line, "His testimony is not grasped through human, generally accepted criteria; nor can it be subjected to them." He speaks of the preaching of the Baptist also as an "appeal to an unprovable authorization through revelation." [15] But these statements can mean more than one thing. If they are to be taken to mean that no evidences can offer more proof than the self-authenticating character of the divine revelation itself and that the proof no matter how extensive can never compel a man to faith, this much has already been granted in a discussion of Christ's witness. Unfortunately, in these and in many other instances the rejection of the evidences for faith goes beyond this observation to involve an absolute and categorical rejection of the verifiable character of revelation considered in itself.

In an extreme denial of the validity of evidences Bultmann's statements are unmatched, and his views are well known. He writes:

> For the truth of his word he [Christ] offers not the slightest guarantees, not even by his miracles, the significance of which is not found in the certification of his word; on the contrary, he explicitly rejects a self-legitimation through miracles.

> The Revealer appears as a man whose claim to be the Son of God is one which he cannot, indeed, must not, prove to the world.

> There are no criteria to establish the legitimacy of claims to revelation, not the trustworthy testimonies of others, not rational or ethical standards, not inner experiences. The object of faith unlocks itself only to faith; faith is the only means of access.[16]

Quite obviously, Bultmann believes that the signs are in no sense a proof, a legitimation of the Gospel, and that the offense of the Gospel is to be found in just this circumstance. But if this is so, why does Jesus dwell upon the witness of the Baptist, of the signs and of the Scripture in chapter five? And why does He conclude that discussion with a profoundly moving reference to the judgment? It may not be replied to these question that the supplementary witnesses or some of them are themselves revelation, although this is true, and therefore invalid as testimony, for

Christ's entire appeal rests upon the observation that although the hearers may not believe Him for His words alone, yet they may believe Him for the witness of the Baptist or of the Scriptures or of the signs. In developing his position Bultmann must assume, in each case erroneously and in contradiction to the actual preaching of the apostles, that the citation of duly authenticated facts ultimately has no significance for the proclamation of the Gospel and that faith, which is admittedly essential for salvation, is unnecessary and in fact impossible if adequate evidence for it is or could be cited. In opposition to Bultmann's position it must be maintained that personal decision is not made impossible by proof and that the miracles are indeed produced as evidence. One cannot help but feel that in regard to the Fourth Gospel at least Bultmann's position is defective.

It must be acknowledged, of course, that the highest evidence for the truth is the truth itself, that the highest proof of revelation is revelation. This has already been accepted in the discussion regarding Christ's ability to bear witness to Himself in chapter three. Nor can there be doubt that true faith in Jesus is impossible without a spiritual perception which exceeds the normal and even the rational facilities of man. This aspect of the human response to revelation will receive further discussion under the witness of the Spirit. Saving knowledge is a knowledge of faith, and this is not identical with the rational acceptance of Christ's claims. At the same time and on the other hand, however, it must also be said that in John's sight a rational acceptance of the evidence is not without a relationship to faith and that the acknowledgment of the supplementary, divine evidences for Christ's claims is not unprofitable for a saving reception of His revelation.

At the very least the miracles point to the divine origin of the one performing them. As Charles Hodge has written:

> The point which miracles are designed to prove is not so much the truth of the doctrines taught as the divine mission of the teacher. . . . What a man teaches may be true, although not divine as to its origin. But when a man presents himself as a messenger of God, whether he is to be received as such or not depends first on the doctrines which he teaches, and, secondly, upon the works which he performs. If he not only teaches doctrines conformed to the nature of God and consistent with the laws of our own constitution, but also performs works which evince divine power, then we know

not only that the doctrines are true, but also that the teacher is sent of God.[17]

In John's case, of course, it must be added as a second value that the miracles also symbolize and communicate the revelation, and thus have importance as an independent verification of the teaching. In them Christ Himself is presented to the hearers. Action and teaching must agree. If there is a discrepancy, either one or both must be untrue, and the Jews have a right to disbelief. Jesus recognizes the truth of this requirement when He observes, "If I am not doing the works of my Father, then do not believe me." And He goes on to add, pointing to the value of the miracles in themselves, "But if I do them, even though you do not believe me, believe the works, that you may know and understand that the Father is in me and I am in the Father" (10:37, 38). The Johannine miracles are not the result of human faith. They are performed to provoke and further it. And this is meaningless unless they have evidential value. There can be no evidence for revelation apart from revelation. But revelation exists in many forms as supplementary evidence for the truth of Jesus' claims.

What then of unbelief? John indicates that this is the result, not of insufficient evidence, but of the darkness of sin which renders the human heart unable to receive either the witness of Jesus or any outward testimony on His behalf. Unbelief is a moral, not a rational problem, and, thus, John deals with it while at the same time insisting on the evidence. One way in which the gospel points to the cause of unbelief is to highlight the inability of men to receive Christ's word, not because the word is meaningless or unconvincing in itself, but because they do not have it already abiding in their hearts (5:38; cf. I John 5:10). Dodd observes that "the Jews do not believe because, not having the word of God in their hearts, they cannot understand His word in the Scriptures, and, not being willing to 'come to' Christ, they do not see the true significance of that which he does." [18] It must not be forgotten, however, that this deficiency is no *mere* deficiency. It is the result of sin. For in chapter eight Jesus links the inability of the Jews to hear His word with the fact that they are children of the devil and thus in bondage to the devil and to sin (verses 34-47). Jesus knows no other bondage than this. In the face of the evidence for His divine claims nothing else can be the cause of unbelief. It is significant that John closes his account of the public ministry in chapter twelve in similar terms, noting that "though he had done so many signs before them, yet they did not believe him" (12:37), and referring by means of the quotations from Isaiah to a spiritual blinding of the eyes and to a spiritual hardening of the heart on the part of unbelieving Israel.

This vital element, a necessary attention to the reality of man's sinful condition, is strikingly absent from the works referred to and quoted above. The omission has equally striking consequences. In Bultmann's case, to take just one example, this primary oversight has led to a substitution of the concept of misunderstanding for the theme of unbelief.[19] Of course, the signs may be misunderstood. And in no case is there ever a total understanding. The people of Galilee expected a physical bread from heaven. But this is not the theme which John makes central. And the reason it is not made central is that misunderstanding is only a secondary effect, an intellectual error, the cause of which is an inability to believe Christ's claims together with the sin which makes such inability an all too real and all too frightening reality. The problem with denying the "proof value" of testimony to Jesus on the human plane is that such denial equates unbelief with finitude and not with sin. And the latter is the Johannine category. Surely Dodd is more correct when he observes concerning the signs: "If they are acknowledged to be real at all, they are acknowledged as 'works of God'; and since they are in fact performed by Jesus, they make His claim self-evident."[20] In appealing to His signs Jesus is appealing to an eternally valid and morally binding testimony.

THE WITNESS OF THE OLD TESTAMENT

Of the three supplementary witnesses to Christ's claims which are cited in chapter five (the Baptist, the signs and Scripture), it is the evidence of the Scripture upon which John most fully dwells and in reference to which he most clearly adjoins the witness of the Father. This witness is not offered in passing as the others. Nor is it overshadowed by others as in the case of John the Baptist (5:36). Instead, the evangelist has allowed Jesus to concentrate upon this testimony and to develop the themes in such a manner that verses thirty-seven through forty-seven emerge as one of the most significant summaries of the importance of Scripture in the gospel. John writes:

> And the Father who sent me has himself borne witness to me. His voice you have never heard, his form you have never seen; and you do not have his word abiding in you, for you do not believe him whom he has sent. You search the Scriptures, because you think that in them you have eternal life; and it is they that bear witness to me; yet you refuse to come to me that you may have life. . . . Do not think that I shall accuse you to the Father; it is Moses who accuses you, on whom you set your hope. If you believed Moses, you would believe me, for he wrote of me. But if you do not believe his writings, how will you believe my words? (5:37-40, 45-47).

In this passage Jesus claims: 1) that the Old Testament Scriptures are fulfilled in Him, 2) that the unbelieving Jews have perverted the Old Testament and misunderstood it, and 3) that the Old Testament itself will accuse the Jews in judgment.

In dealing with this testimony it must be remembered as a matter of primary importance that Christ's appeal to the Scriptures was an appeal to the highest and ultimately the only authority within Judaism and that the authority of the Old Testament was equally acknowledged within the Christian Church. In the disputes between Church and Synagogue in the early years of the expansion of the Gospel, and even afterwards, the witness of the Scriptures to Jesus of Nazareth by way of prophecy had played a central role. They were the one acknowledged revelation, the word of God; it is even in agreement with the widespread acknowledgment of their authority that at an earlier date Jesus draws attention to them (cf. 10:35).

1. John begins with the basic assurance that the Old Testament Scriptures are fulfilled in Jesus Christ. In the Fourth Gospel the evangelist values the Old Testament Scriptures, like the witness of the Baptist and like the witness of the signs, not, first of all, for their value in themselves, but primarily for the witness which they bear to Jesus. This is a general characteristic of the gospel, and it is seen quite clearly in a number of references to Old Testament personalities and events as well as in Christ's explicit statements in John 5. Moses did not give the true bread from heaven; it is the Father who gives true bread, and that true bread is Christ (6:32, 35). Moses lifted up the serpent

in the wilderness for healing; but Jesus is the One who is to be lifted up for the salvation of the world (3:14, 15). John brings all of these items and others into a relationship to Jesus Christ and indicates in many instances that he and he alone is the fulfillment of the Old Testament hopes and expectations.

It would be very surprising if this basic orientation did not also lead John to include in the gospel certain scriptural quotations which were believed to have a specific fulfillment in the events of Christ's life and ministry, especially since the practice of arguing from Scripture had been basic to the early proclamation of the Gospel and undoubtedly exercised a vital if not a governing influence upon the ordering of the tradition. It is true, as commentators have frequently pointed out, that John's interest in the Old Testament does not exactly duplicate the interest of the Synoptic writers. John's quotations are less frequent. He depends upon them less. But if this line of observation is to be kept in true perspective, it cannot be forgotten that even though the quotations are less frequent they are still quite freely used and that John's deviation from the Synoptic pattern lies more in his emphasis than in his presuppositions or beliefs.

In the course of the narrative John introduces sixteen direct or nearly direct quotations from the Old Testament (1:23; 2:17; 6:31, 45; 7:42; 10:34; 12:13, 15, 38, 40; 13:18; 15:25; 19:24, 28-29, 36, 37) to which may be added three other passages (1:51; 7:38; 19:1-3) which do not contain a direct quotation but which so closely suggest an Old Testament text that the reference may be supposed to have been apparent to many of the readers of the gospel. This material is drawn, as in the earlier gospels, largely from the messianic psalms and from the prophets, notably Isaiah, and in an indirect manner from the Pentateuch. Nearly all of these references are prefaced by some standard formula of introduction: "as it is written," "to fulfill the Scripture," "that the Scripture might be fulfilled," "as the Scripture has said," and others. Thus, although John is less prone to Old Testament quotation than the Synoptic writers—Mark alone has nearly fifty allusions to Old Testament passages—his procedure in regard to direct scriptural quotation is not much different from their own.

John believes that the "scripture cannot be broken" (10:35) and that specific Old Testament prophecies are indeed fulfilled in Christ. It is within all probability that in the use of this material John is drawing upon a well-entrenched tradition. Nevertheless,

John seems remarkably independent of the texts employed by the previous evangelists and chooses his quotations (often only allusions) to meet the theological demands of his narration.

To stop at this point, however, would be to fall short of the Johannine doctrine of the Old Testament. For although John does not abstain from quoting proof texts, still he goes beyond the procedure of the earlier evangelists to stress the importance of the witness which the Scriptures *in their totality* are rendering to Jesus Christ. This perspective emerges most clearly in Christ's references to three representative Old Testament personalities: Abraham (the first and the greatest of the patriarchs), Moses (the mediator of the law), and Isaiah (the most important of the prophets). It can hardly be regarded as an accident that these are the only three Old Testament personalities mentioned by name in connection with the ministry of Jesus.

In chapter eight (verses 33-59) the name of *Abraham* is introduced into a spirited debate between Jesus and the Jews which revolves in consequence around the subject of their spiritual descent. The Jews claim that they are children of Abraham (verses 33 and 39). Jesus recognizes that they are indeed descended (physically) from Abraham (verse 37), but He denies that they are Abraham's true children in the spiritual sense, for if they were his children they would act like Abraham. That is, they would believe in Christ. Against this background and with some irony John places an observation upon the Jews' actual parentage ("You are of your father the devil," verse 44) and contrasts the confusion of the Jews regarding Christ's true origins ("Are we not right in saying that you are a Samaritan and have a demon?" verse 48) with the fact that He occupied eternity with God ("Before Abraham was, I am," verse 58). The section closes with the observation that "Abraham rejoiced that he was to see my day; he saw it and was glad" (verse 56).

The "seeing" of Abraham, upon which his witness depends and with reference to which the conversation terminates, is the point of greatest interest. What is intended by his "seeing"? It is very doubtful whether this can be an observation which is temporally coincident with the events of Christ's life, as Godet and Bernard maintain,[21] for the point of the argument is that it is Christ who is co-existent with Abraham and not Abraham who is co-existent with Christ. Moreover, such a seeing would be opposed to the normative Johannine usage according to which seeing denotes a form of spiritual perception. This seeing may be a seeing by faith, as Calvin teaches and Westcott,[22] but it is quite likely, more likely in view of rabbinical beliefs, that the reference is to a special revelation of the ministry of Christ given to Abraham in his own day. This is the view of Hoskyns, Schlatter, and Barrett.[23] As a result of such a seeing, whether by a special revelation or by faith, the emphasis falls entirely upon the expectant character of Abraham's experience and upon the fulfillment of the promises in Christ to whom the faith of Abraham and the faith of the other Old Testament figures bear eloquent testimony.

The same point of view is evident in the references to *Moses*. In this case John teaches that just as the expectations and experiences of the patriarchs were incomplete in themselves but were made complete in Christ, so also is Christ the fulfillment of all the statutes and the figures of the law. Two examples of this Johannine teaching have already been suggested. Christ is the true bread from heaven of which the manna given through Moses in the wilderness was only a type. And similarly, Christ is the fulfillment of the symbol of the serpent raised in the wilderness for the healing of the people. A further example may be found in Christ's discussions of the Sabbath, in which the seventh day is subordinated to the ministry of Christ and is set aside rightly for His acts of healing (7:22, 23). John's own statement of Christ's relation to the law is found as early as the prologue— "For the law was given through Moses; grace and truth came through Jesus Christ" (1:17). Jesus observes in the discussion of witnesses in chapter five, "If you believed Moses, you would believe me, for he wrote of me. But if you do not believe his writings, how will you believe my words?" (5:46, 47). The importance of the Mosaic legislation is in its preparatory character, and in this character it points to Christ.

John's references to *Isaiah* are only two, but each is significant and each occurs with reference to a passage from his writings. The first is found at the beginning of the gospel in the familiar designation of the Baptist—"I am the voice of one crying in the wilderness, 'Make straight the way of the Lord' " (1:23; cf. Isa. 40:3). The second occurs at the end of the public ministry in connection with the prophecy that Christ's coming would be met by unbelief. In this instance John follows the statement regarding the blindness and the deafness of the Jews with the summary of Isaiah's prophetic expectation of the Christ, in which the prophet emerges as a witness, even an eyewitness, of Christ's glory. "Isaiah said this because he saw his glory and spoke of him" (12:41). The reference in this verse can only be to Isaiah's vision of the Lord sitting upon the throne high and lifted up (Isaiah 6), which John has understood as a vision of the Christ, and to the directly spoken words of Christ which Isaiah heard in that vision and which are reported immediately beforehand in the gospel (12:40; Isa. 6:10).

In these instances John's understanding of the Old Testament witness to Jesus Christ goes beyond an interest in the specific prophecies which were explicitly fulfilled in Christ, although this was also a part of the Johannine understanding as has been indicated, to fasten upon a comprehensive fulfillment of the Old Testament expectations in their entirety. This view is quite similar to that of the epistle to the Hebrews and is not at all different from John's basic insistence that all revelation, including all of the preparatory revelation of the Old Testament, is really one revelation with its true center and organic unity in Christ. On John's use of the Old Testament witness Westcott comments perceptively, "The writer of the Fourth Gospel is penetrated throughout—more penetrated perhaps than any other writer of the New Testament—with the spirit of the Old. The interpretations which he gives and records, naturally and without explanation or enforcement, witness to a method of dealing with the old Scriptures which is of wide application. He brings them all into connection with Christ. He guides his readers to their abiding meaning, *which cannot be broken;* he warns the student against trusting to the letter, while he assures him that no fragment of the teaching of *the Word of God* is without its use. And in doing this he shows also how the scope of revelation grows with the growth of men. Without the basis of the Old Testament, without the fullest acceptance of the unchanging divinity of the Old Testament, the Gospel of St. John is an insoluble riddle." [24]

2. The statement of Jesus in John 5 also indicates that the unbelieving Jews have perverted the Old Testament and misunderstood it. The perversion of the Old Testament which the evangelist sees the Jewish people to be making lies along two lines. In the first place, the Jews have perverted, not only the Scriptures, but the whole of their religion and even their messianic expectations by taking these great privileges as a religious

possession of their own. In erring along these lines they become
defensive and fail to see that the privileges given to them, far
from becoming their own possession, actually make the people
themselves the possession of God and impose upon them the demand to recognize God wherever and whenever He reveals Himself. In the second place, the Jews err in their belief that the
Scriptures possess life in themselves and are themselves the source
of man's salvation. In failing to perceive that only God is the
source of life, they fail to look to Him even in the Scriptures and
are unable to recognize the incarnation of life in Jesus when
Jesus Christ appears.

The evangelist provides many examples of this first perversion
of the Scriptures. The Jews trusted to their law, which was
handed down to Moses and Aaron and the people at Sinai, yet
they were unable to see that it was not a finished revelation,
sufficient in itself, which they possessed but an unfinished revelation which pointed forward to a greater reality which they
did not possess. Christ Himself indicates this truth in chapter
seven by pointing to two conflicting requirements of the law—
that no work should be done upon the Sabbath and that a child
should be circumcised on the eighth day after birth which would
often be performed upon the Sabbath (7:22-24). He then argues
that in this ambiguous situation even the rulers recognized that
the letter of the law would not suffice and obeyed the commandment which was needful for the child. How much more then
should they permit the works of Jesus who is able to make a
man's whole body whole (verse 23)? A further example is the
case of Abraham which has been discussed above (8:33-59).
The Jews think that they possess him by virtue of their descent
("Abraham is our father," verse 39) and thus are entitled to all
the blessings which Abraham enjoyed. What they fail to see is
that Abraham looked forward to the Messiah and that they are
his true children only to the extent to which they also look forward to His coming and accept Him when He comes.

The supreme example of this self-righteous, contented possession of the law is found in the Jews' conversation with the man
who had been born blind. In this conflict the Jews put their confidence in the fact that "we know that God has spoken to Moses"
(9:29) and in the belief that "we are [his] disciples" (9:28).
Against these statements the man who had been healed points
to the unquestioned fact of the healing itself and concludes that

"if this man were not from God, he could do nothing" (9:33). In making the Old Testament law their own the Jews pervert its meaning, for they fail to see that it is precisely to *Jesus* that the former revelation bears its witness.

It is an irony of the Jews' procedure at this point, clearly seen by John, that in making Scripture something which they possess and can parcel out at their discretion they actually lose whatever claim they rightly have to it and end by renouncing their own past and the legitimate benefits which fall to them as Jews. This element emerges as a tragic undercurrent at Christ's trial, at which in their violent rejection of the One to whom the law and the prophets bear witness the leaders cry out saying, "We have no king but Caesar" (19:15). Ironically, they speak as Romans in rejecting Jesus and forfeit their God-given benefits as Jews.

Secondly, the Jews also err in their persuasion that the Scriptures are themselves the source of life. Jesus observes as a matter of factual information in the context of chapter five that "you search the Scriptures, because you think that in them you have eternal life" (verse 39). There can be no doubt that here Jesus is speaking in the indicative and not in the imperative, although the verb may be either, to describe a condition of fact and the erroneous belief that accompanied it. It is not that the Jews are exhorted to investigate the Scriptures. The rabbis were exemplary in this pursuit. Rather they are to see that such an investigation rightly conducted leads a man to Christ and that the chief obstacle to this perception is the erroneous Jewish belief that the Torah itself possesses life.[25]

John does not think for a moment, however, that all that is needed for a correct understanding of the Torah is a new exegesis in the form of Christian midrash or even the perception that the Scriptures are a preparation for a greater revelation in terms of an acute messianic expectation. What is needed is a new birth and with it a different way of life. The decisive passage in this regard is the conversation between Jesus and Nicodemus, a man who, as a Pharisee and as a ruler, is a representative figure of the Jews. In this context a Jewish reader would expect a rabbinical debate, a discussion of the messianic character, or something similar. Instead, the situation is no sooner introduced than Jesus moves the discussion to a higher and more spiritual plane. Jesus answers Nicodemus, "Truly, truly, I say to you, unless one is born anew, he cannot see the kingdom of God" (3:3). This indicates that the cause of the Jewish perversion of the Scriptures, like their inability to understand the signs and their hostility to the message of the Baptist, is to be traced, in the ultimate analysis, to a lack of spiritual life. Their deficiency is not intellectual but moral, and it is closely connected with their sin. In chapter five this vital deficiency is said to express itself, not only in unbelief, but also negatively in a lack of the divine love (verse 42) and positively in the longing for human glory instead of that glory which comes alone from God (verse 44).

At the same time it must not be forgotten that to John there is still a very positive value to the Scriptures. For the lack of spiritual life on the part of the unbelieving Jews together with the understanding of the Torah which results from it does not change the truth of Scripture nor alter its value as an evidence for the claims of Jesus Christ. The Scripture is still a witness, and rightly understood it leads a man to Christ. Jesus says, "If you believed Moses, you would believe me, for he wrote of me" (5:46). As Strachan observes, "Jesus does not say that intensive study of the Old Testament must take a subordinate place in the lives of those who are his disciples; but that such study properly understood, actually should lead men to come to himself and tell men more of himself." [26]

It is also possible that John has intended the story of the calling of Nathanael as an example of the possibility of recognizing Jesus on the basis of a study of the Torah. It is to be remembered, first, that in rabbinical lore the fig tree, under one of which Nathanael had been sitting, was the tree of Torah study and, second, that Nathanael is expressly identified as an exemplary Jewish figure, "an Israelite indeed, in whom is no guile" (1:47). Such a one would be attentive to the words of the law, and Philip appeals to him on just these lines. Philip says, "Come and see" (1:46); that is, come and test whether Jesus is the one "of whom Moses in the law and also the prophets wrote" (1:45). Nathanael replies after seeing Jesus, "Rabbi, you are the Son of God! You are the King of Israel" (1:49). In the light of John's preference for double meanings and symbolic events it does not seem unlikely that Nathanael provides an illustration of Jesus' saying, reported later, that a true belief in Moses would lead men to a saving recognition of Himself (5:46). In such a view John approaches closely what the reformers called the perspicuity of Scripture.

If all of this is true before Christ's death and resurrection, the events which provide the clue for the correct understanding of the Old Testament, then it is equally or more true afterwards. If unbelief is inexcusable before Christ's passion for those who know the Scriptures, it is more inexcusable now that the Scriptures are fulfilled. Since this is the perspective in history from which the fourth evangelist is writing, it is difficult to doubt that John also reflects this truth as the belief and practice of the early Christian preaching when he allows Jesus to cite the Scriptures in this personal, compelling challenge to belief.

3. Jesus also teaches in chapter five that it is the Old Testament itself which will accuse the Jews in judgment. Having spoken of the Jewish perversion of the Scriptures and of their desire for the praise of men to which their lack of spiritual life has led them, Jesus now goes on to unveil the danger to which they are exposed. This danger is the danger of judgment, a present judgment, not by Christ whose words they refused to accept, but by the very law they do accept and which they trust for their salvation. Jesus says, "It is Moses who accuses you, on whom you set your hope" (5:45).

This statement together with Christ's claim that He will not accuse the Jews before His Father is not to be taken as conflicting with the statement in chapter twelve that "he who rejects me and does not receive my sayings has a judge; the word that I have spoken will be his judge on the last day" (verse 48), nor with the claim in chapter five that the Father has given the Son "authority to execute judgment, because he is the Son of man" (verse 27). The topic under discussion in chapter five is not the identity of the judge but the identity of the accuser, the witness for the prosecution in contemporary legal terminology. The Scripture will be one accuser. But there will be others also. The signs will present an accusation. And so will the witness of the Baptist. Even Christ's coming will be a cause for judgment for those who disregard it (3:19). In the case at hand, Jesus dwells upon the accusing character of the Mosaic legislation simply because it is upon the law that the Jews base their hopes for everlasting life. The Jews do not actually believe this law, despite their protests, and they certainly do not understand it; for had they understood it they would inevitably have believed in Jesus Christ. In a similar vein Eliezer ben Jacob observed on the law and judgment: "He who does one precept gains for himself one advocate; and he who commits one transgression gains for himself one accuser" (Pirkē Aboth 4:13).

The final verses of chapter five develop the thesis of verse 45 by speaking of two ways, the way of unbelief which begins with a rejection of the true meaning of the Mosaic Scriptures and ends in an inevitable rejection of Jesus, and the way of belief which begins with a true understanding of the Old Testament and ends with a saving recognition of the Christ. As Godet notes, both of these propositions "are founded on the principle that the two covenants are the development of one and the same fundamental thought and have the same moral substance." [27] It is a corollary of this unalterable connection that one phase of the divine revelation may not be played off against another. All revelation is directed toward the form of Jesus Christ, and all revelation leads to faith in Him (cf. Heb. 1:1-3). To fail to perceive this connection is to fail to understand the revelation or, which is worse, to disregard or disbelieve it.

THE NATURE OF THE EVIDENCE

The divine testimony to Jesus Christ centers upon three supplementary witnesses: the witness of the Baptist, the witness of the signs, and the witness of Scripture. All three involve the direct and supernatural activity of God, and all three may, therefore, be described as aspects of the Father's own testimony to the person and the teaching of the Son. The Baptist's witness is that of a prophet and thus of the *prophetic word*. John is particularly careful to cite this witness accurately, leaving an impression of great respect for the witness of the Baptist as an established historical datum.

The witness of the signs represents the *acted word*. The identity of the supplementary witnesses with revelation is particularly evident in this second type of witness, for the signs are performed by Jesus and have the communication of His glory as their object.

The final witness is that of the Old Testament Scriptures which is the *written word*. This witness is a preparatory witness, like the testimony of the Baptist. But although an incomplete and expectant revelation, it is, nevertheless, a distinct and historically validated entity which John considers adequate to lead a man to faith in Jesus. In this elaboration of the Christian evidences, all of which have faith and decision as their object, the student of the gospel is certainly not far removed from the missionary apologetics of the early Church or part of it.

In all of the cases so elaborated revelation bears witness to revelation, but this is not exactly the same thing as saying that revelation as a fixed entity bears witness to itself. Such a statement would be meaningless. What is involved in the supplementary witnesses to Jesus is a great and widely significant variety in the modes of revelation, all of which focus upon the figure of Jesus who is both the author of all revelation, as the Logos, and the subject of all revelation as the incarnate Christ. The prophetic revelation, the acted revelation and the written revelation point to Him. These, as seen individually, but especially as seen together, constitute external (as opposed to the internal witness of the Spirit), visible, often audible and, in every sense, corroborative testimony to the person of Jesus and to the meaning of His ministry. They constitute the fullest evidence for His claims which can be given.

It has become increasingly apparent in the preceding study, however, that it is not just as evidence that the supplementary witnesses are significant. They are not mere mechanical proofs. They are revelation, and as revelation they bear a direct and not merely an indirect relationship to Christ. This means, as John indicates, that they assist the receptive individual to understand Him. In the case of John the Baptist this understanding is to be seen pre-eminently in Christ's identification. The one pointed out by John is the sin-bearing Lamb, the pre-existent One, the Son of God.

The signs also assist in understanding Jesus, for they provide not only a revelation of His glory but at the same time an acted illustration of His teaching. As seen in chapter three of this study, the acts are so closely related to the words of Christ that the signs may quite correctly be considered the Johannine equivalent of His parables.

Finally, Scripture also assists in the understanding of Christ's person. This is true first by anticipation. It was seen, for instance, that Nathanael's understanding of the Old Testament is probably to be understood as teaching that the study of the Torah provides the categories by which the Messiah was to be recognized and prepares the mind to receive Him when He comes. At the same time the Scriptures also contribute to an understanding of Jesus subsequent to the event. Here the witness of the Old Testament by way of prophecy and by suggestive figures plays an important role. It is even true that the Old Testament becomes more important subsequent to the incarnation than before, for Christ's life, death, and resurrection are the keys for understanding it. The past and the present revelation thus illuminate and interpret each other.

The permanent character of the supplementary witnesses is also striking. It was particularly evident in a study of the Baptist's witness that the forerunner's testimony was especially preserved for the effect of its bearing on the present. John testifies for the readers of the gospel. His witness has a permanent validity. But this is true, not only of the Baptist's witness, but also of the witness of the Old Testament Scriptures. Their abiding relevance is to be seen not only in the eternally significant fact of their fulfillment, but also in the fact that through a study of Scripture men may still be led to a personal and abiding faith in Jesus. At first sight the witness of the signs might be thought to be an exception. But these abide not only in the Scriptures of the New Testament—a point which John at his position in history could hardly emphasize—but also as an ever present reality in the Church, in the sacraments which the signs prefigure, and in the present power of the Logos, creating faith and governing and preserving believers in the Christian Gospel. In this way God the Father sets His seal upon the Son (6:27; cf. also 3:33), not only during the period of the incarnation but also during the period of the ongoing expansion of the Church. This is to say, first, that the Father is ever active in the sacraments and the preaching of the Church, validating the claims of Christ and, second, that Christ Himself is present, manifesting Himself through those sacraments and through that preaching to those who believe. This type of persuasion is as far removed from mere legal evidence as a person is removed from a document, but it is a persuasion which utilizes evidence rather than rejecting it.

Finally, it must be said that it is only when the evidential value of the supplementary witness is recognized in all its seriousness that the reality of judgment can be perceived and its connection with revelation be maintained. The judgment threatens not only because of disbelief but because the unbelief of men is revealed precisely as their unbelief when they are confronted with the evidence for the claims of Jesus Christ. The failure to believe is revealed, not as misunderstanding or doubt—these are stripped away—but as a willful rejection of Jesus and His claims which is at its core an expression of human sin. For this reason the supplementary witnesses must also be considered as a trial, a temptation, an opportunity for belief or disbelief, with all the danger of an immediate and an impending judgment. This trial together with their value as evidences and as an aspect of the revelation of Christ's person, constitute the value of the supplementary witnesses to the evangelist and a more than adequate reason for their careful elaboration in the gospel.

Chapter 5

The Human Testimony to Jesus Christ

THE TESTIMONY OF THE APOSTLES

It has already been noted in dealing with the revelation of Jesus and the verification of His claims by the Father that John is creative in his use of the witness terminology. John is dealing with questions which were not asked by the earlier evangelists, and he is using the witness terminology in a way which has no parallel in the other New Testament writings. John's writings are unique in their treatment of Jesus' witness and the witness of the Father. This is not entirely true when the evangelist deals with human witness, the witness of the apostles and of other men. In dealing with human testimony to Jesus Christ, particularly the testimony of the apostles, John is actually guided in part by his understanding of the apostolic age.

Some of the characteristics of the age preceding the writing of the gospel have already come to light in a discussion of the Lukan literature. It was argued at some length in chapter two that in Luke and Acts a special role is given to the apostles as to those who had been present with Jesus from the time of the baptism by John to the final ascension into heaven and who had been specifically chosen by the resurrected Lord to verify the facts of His life and ministry, particularly His death and resurrection. Luke uses the word *martys* to denote a member of this particular body of men and, with the possible exception of Stephen, uses it exclusively for that end. It must be remembered, therefore, that when John applies the term witness to the apostles he is not without precedent in earlier Christian literature.

Nor is the special role of the apostles confined solely to Luke's writings. It would be difficult to deny that the twelve occupy a special position even in Mark and Matthew, and the whole tenor of the Pauline epistles, in so far as they touch upon the apostolate, presupposes an official and established, one might almost say a legal, institution. Thus, when Paul is at pains to defend his own apostleship in the opening chapters of Galatians, he does so by identifying himself with those who were generally acknowledged as apostles and by maintaining that his own apostleship rested upon an identical foundation with theirs (Gal. 1:1, 11, 12). In these verses as in Romans 1:1; I Corinthians 9:1; 15:7, 8, Paul does not use the word witness of the apostolate as is the case in Acts, but he does presuppose an authoritative apostolic office and does so in a way which is in essential harmony with the Synoptic gospels and with the Lukan history of the early Church. In fact, in spite of his insistence upon an authority equal to and independent of the twelve apostles, Paul is not averse to referring to his experience of "receiving" and "delivering" the tradition, delivered to the Gentile congregations and presumably received in an official character from the first apostles as they received it from the Lord (I Cor. 11:23; 15:3).

There can be little doubt, then, that in the early years of the Christian Church the apostles did exercise an important and widely acknowledged role as verifiers of the Gospel tradition and that this function must be regarded as the background for whatever comments John makes upon their office in his development of the witness terminology.

These conclusions are so apparent that they are generally accepted by all scholars who take the witness of the New Testament to the existence of the apostolic office seriously. Thus, Rengstorf in his article for the Kittel *Theological Dictionary of the New Testament* speaks of the two qualifications for apostleship, to be an eyewitness of the resurrected Lord and to be commissioned by Him directly, placing the greatest emphasis upon the divine commission. In a longer study he finds a pre-history of the Christian apostleship in Judaism.[1] Brox expresses nearly the same view adding only that the apostle must also be one who has accepted the commission bestowed upon him in his encounter with the risen Lord.[2] Bichon, Brunner, M. Barth, Casey and Cullmann write along similar but not identical lines, and Holl takes the function of the apostle so seriously that he is even willing to argue, although probably erroneously, that the phrase *martys tou Theou,* derived from I Corinthians 15:15 (*pseudomartyres tou Theou*), was a technical term for one who had seen the risen Lord.[3] Strathmann places the authority of the apostolate alongside the authority of Christ and of the Old Testament as one of the three formative factors in the development of the life and doctrine of the primitive Church.[4] And Lietzmann inquires rhetorically, "What was the position of the original apostles? May we still regard them as the real founders and the recognized authorities of the Church? Most certainly; and their importance is clear enough from the way in which Paul had to struggle at a later date. They were indeed not only the guarantors and vehicles of the tradition, but also they had been appointed to sit on twelve thrones, under the presidency of the Son of Man, and judge the twelve tribes of Israel in the Messianic Kingdom." [5]

On the whole it is only among the most ardent of the form critics that one hears a discordant note, and even here the tendency is not so much to deny the primacy of the apostles as to negate the significance of their witness in guiding and controlling the tradition. From the standpoint of the form critics there is really little choice; for the acknowledgment of a functioning apostolate is required by the evidence, while at the same time the admission of a normative and controlling factor within the Christian community is basically incompatible with the vision of a spiritually democratic Church, producing the material of the New Testament out of its own existential and eschatologically oriented experience. A sophisticated example of an attempted solution of this dilemma is provided by Nineham, who admits the role of eyewitnesses at the source level of the earliest gospel texts, but denies that it broke into, corrected or controlled the tradition from that time forward.[6]

In the light of such viewpoints the evidence of the Fourth Gospel to the role of the apostles is of great significance. For if John was writing toward the end of the apostolic age (*circa* A.D. 90) at a time when the earlier gospels and the Pauline epistles had already been written and had begun to circulate in their present form and if John reflects a viewpoint in respect to the apostles which is similar to the earlier texts, then the role of the apostles in guiding and authenticating the tradition is presumably greater and of longer duration than is or can be generally admitted by the form critical school. And the gospels must be of greater historical reliability than they admit. At the same time, simply because he is writing somewhat later, John may be expected to add to the material from the earlier sources along the lines of what can be called a theological reflection upon the role actually played by the apostles in the primitive Church and thus to provide information about their role in terms of a theological evaluation.

It may be mentioned as a point of departure for the study of the apostolate in John that the disciples received a direct, divine commission, an authorization for their task, and exist as a unique body distinct from those who follow them. This is evident in a general but most decisive way in John seventeen. In this carefully constructed petition Jesus prays first for Himself (verses 1-5), second for His disciples (verses 6-19), and third for the Church which will come into being through their witness (verses 20-26), dwelling at greatest length upon the disciples as those who have been specifically chosen for their work by God (verse 6), who have received the word originally given to Himself (verses 8 and 14), and who have been sent into the world (verse 18) that others might believe through their communication (verse 20). This three-part outline is greatly to be preferred, as in Luther, Calvin, Bengel, H. J. Holtzmann, Schlatter, M. Barth and Cullmann, to the two-part schema devised by Bultmann.[7] It sets out the line of descent for the tradition in terms of *Heilsgeschichte* and establishes the primary and normative role of the apostles in that process. Cullmann notes correctly that "no writing of the New Testament emphasizes so much as the Fourth Gospel the continuation of the work of Christ incarnate in the Church. . . . But it is this very Gospel which distinguishes clearly between the continuation by the apostles, which is part of the central period, and the continuation by the post-apostolic Church. The high-priestly prayer (chap. 17) establishes this line of descent: Christ—the apostles—the post-apostolic Church."[8]

It is also interesting to note that "witnesses" appear alongside of the "saints" in Revelation 17:6, in which verse the distinction is not, as many assume, between all Christians and the martyrs—both are said to have shed blood for Jesus Christ—but between Christians in general and those who have a special role as witnesses, that is to say, between the apostles and those who constitute the Church.

The unique position of the apostles implied in John 17 is given body by the evangelist's awareness of their calling, indicated by reference to their sending. In 20:21 the idea of a divine commission of the disciples mentioned first in 17:18 is repeated to the disciples directly, subsequent to the resurrection— "As the Father has sent me, even so send I you"—and the final chapter of the gospel, whether by the hand of the original author or by the authorities who add the postscript (21:24, 25), certainly has the rehabilitation of Peter and the commissioning of the disciples to the task of world evangelism in view.

With the idea of a divine commission goes also the necessity of being an eyewitness as in Luke and Acts. Like Luke, John stresses that the disciples can fulfill their function because they have been eyewitnesses of all the events of Jesus' ministry. "And you also are witnesses, because you have been with me from the beginning" (15:27; cf. Luke 1:2; Acts 1:21, 22). In this instance the witness of the disciples is placed alongside the witness of Christ's words (verse 22), of Christ's works (verse 24) and the witness of the Spirit (verse 26), the testimony of the disciples having its unique significance in that they alone are able to verify the facts of His life and ministry. Every incident of Christ's life observed by the disciples and recorded in the gospel is an example of this activity, but on some occasions the event is too significant for the Christian faith for John merely to assume this function. At Christ's crucifixion, for instance, John calls particular attention to the spear thrust, guaranteeing Christ's literal and physical death, and to the one who observed it, whose "testimony is true" and who "knows that he tells the truth" (19:35). Similarly, in the resurrection account it would appear that John has so structured the incidents that the evidence for the resurrection rests, not primarily upon the women, although Mary Magdalene is a witness to the opened sepulcher, but upon the testimony of the two chief apostles, Peter and John, who are the first to look into the grave. They verify that the tomb was empty. The eyewitness ability of the disciples to verify the facts of Jesus' life is given added significance in the formal statement by which John concludes the Easter narrative. "Now Jesus did many other signs *in the presence of the disciples,* which are not written in this book; but these are written that you may believe that Jesus is the Christ, the Son of God, and that believing you may have life in his name" (20:30, 31).

On the basis of the evidence for a special position of the apostles in the gospel, it is correct to say that John ascribes an importance to the apostles as the sole authenticating agents of the tradition which is in all essentials at one with the picture of them in Luke-Acts and in the Pauline epistles. The apostles are eyewitnesses of the events they verify, and they are specifically chosen for that purpose by the risen Lord. It must not be forgotten *vis à vis* the form critics that this viewpoint is still maintained even near the end of the first Christian century and presumably in Asia Minor where Bultmann at least chooses to discover an exclusively Hellenistic Christianity.[9]

It must be added to this analysis that John's evaluation of the apostolic office also goes beyond what is expressed by Luke and Paul, for just as John has reflected theologically upon many of the great doctrines of Christianity, so has he reflected theologically upon the apostolic institution. This is suggested quite vividly from the perspective of the present study by an interesting observation upon John's use of the word witness in 15:27. Here Jesus speaks of the disciples as witnesses of the events of His ministry, utilizing the participle, much in the way that Luke refers to them as *martyres*. Does this mean that John is departing from his normative usage according to which "witness" has a primary meaning in terms of revelation? Is John merely reflecting the Lukan terminology? Or does John in fact conceive of the apostolic witness in all its historical reality as belonging within the sphere of his greater witness concepts? There are numerous reasons for believing that the latter idea is the correct one.

In the first place, Christ is pictured as commissioning the disciples in terms which parallel his own commission from the Father. He says, "As the Father has sent (*apostellein*) me, even so I send (*pempein*) you" (20:21). Both verbs are used of the Son's commission from the Father, the former in 3:17, 34; 5:36, 38; 6:29, 57; 7:29; 8:42; 11:42; 17:3, 8, 21, 23, 25, the latter in 4:34; 5:23, 24, 30, 37; 6:38, 39, 44; 7:16, 28. And both are used of the disciples (4:38; 13:20; 17:18). It is not to be thought, then, that Christ distinguishes between His being sent and their commission, but that He identifies the two, doing so in such a way that their mission becomes an extension of His own. The emphasis lies primarily upon the mission of the Son and secondarily upon the mission of the disciples. As "sent ones" they extend His testimony. Hence, the mission of the disciples is Christ's mission, not their own. Westcott writes that the "disciples receive no new commission, but carry out his. . . . They are not (in this respect) his envoys, but in a secondary degree envoys of the Father." [10] If the disciples are termed witnesses against this background, there is every reason to associate their witness, to one degree or another, with the revelation which has been manifest in Christ and to relate their authority as bearers of the tradition to His own.

The same perspective is also indicated in some of Christ's teachings about the Holy Spirit. In 20:22, just after Jesus has commissioned the disciples to His own mission, Jesus breathes upon them and thereby imparts to them His Spirit. It is doubtful whether in this context the gift of Christ's Spirit may simply be identified with the outpouring of the Holy Spirit at Pentecost; for Pentecost is an event which is repeated in the experience of all believers, and in this incident there is apparently a special reference to those whom Christ commissioned as apostles and to their special service. John distinguishes it from the later event by referring to "holy spirit," without the article, instead of to "the Holy Spirit" and by associating it in the closest possible manner with their task—"As the Father has sent me, even so I send you" (verse 21). The Spirit imparted in this way will lead the disciples into an understanding of "all the truth" (14:26; 16: 12-15). And their witness will be true because truth is the primary characteristic of the Spirit (14:17; 15:26; 16:13).

Now if this special impartation of Christ's spirit and the fact that they are witnesses means anything in the case of the disciples, it must mean as a matter of basic importance that spiritual understanding is added to the eyewitness reporting and the selection by Christ as the third characteristic of the apostolate. In this John goes beyond the other New Testament writers. The apostle is not merely one who has seen and has chosen to bear witness, however important that may be. He is also one who has seen and understood. This theme is an important one in John. The witness of the apostles as apostles involves an understanding made possible by the Spirit and communicated to the disciples subsequent to the resurrection. By that gift they are enabled, not merely to transmit the facts of Christ's life and of His suffering, but also to transmit the true meaning of those facts and their true significance for the continuing proclamation of the Gospel in the Church. The fact is a sign of something which lies deeper. The earthly things are historical realities in which heavenly things have been revealed. John's own perception of the spiritual meaning of the events of Christ's ministry plays such a significant role in the actual composition of the narrative that it is quite correct to speak in this sense, as some writers have done, of the originality of the Johannine revelation.

The special gift of the Spirit which is associated with the special ministry of the apostles is also of great significance for an understanding of Jesus' revelation, for since the Spirit is the Spirit of Christ it means that Jesus did not cease His ministry of revelation because His earthly life was ended. Rather did He continue it through His Spirit through the chosen representatives to whom He is united by faith and in whom the Spirit dwells. Through them His work continues. This does not mean that they may amplify upon or correct His earthly revelation, for Christ's life and ministry are still the center of all revelation and its full expression. They are to witness to the truth concerning *Him*. It does not mean that their transmission of the events of His ministry will be mechanical. For His Spirit will be testifying in their testimony, and this is a personal revelation. What it does mean is that Jesus as the exalted Lord is Lord of the tradition, its source, its object and its active principle. The apostles have no independent value in themselves. Even as eyewitnesses they have no value until they understand the meaning of what they have observed, and this they do not understand until after the resurrection and the gift of Jesus' Spirit. The importance of the apostles lies in the fact that through them Christ Himself continues to testify. Their mission is His mission. Their witness is His witness. As M. Barth observes:

> The testimony of the apostles is persuasive and successful because their testimony, their person, and their function as witnesses are confirmed by the same Lord for whom they are eye-witnesses and by the same truth of which they are persuaded.[11]

And Cullmann notes with particular reference to the Fourth Gospel:

> Behind the apostles' tradition of the deeds and words of the incarnate Christ stands the exalted Lord himself, according to decisive affirmations in the New Testament. The consciousness of being an organ of Jesus Christ, who as the exalted Lord creates the post-Easter tradition about his own

earthly work, is once more particularly apparent in the Gospel of John (14:26), but the *whole* Gospel tradition is inspired by it.[12]

It would be correct to say that in the apostolic mission Jesus is once again active in revelation as the Logos (the Spirit), confirming and interpreting the events of the period of His incarnation, just as He had been active in revelation as the Logos before the incarnation, preparing for it through the revelation of the Old Testament Scriptures. The works done by the disciples and the words spoken by them are really the words and the works of Christ, just as the words and works of Christ during His earthly life were the words and the actions of the Father.

This means, of course, that God's revelation is also to be seen, not only in the Old Testament and not only in the person of Jesus in His incarnate form, but also in the witness of the apostles during the apostolic age. The words of the apostles are themselves a part of the divine revelation. And they are themselves revelation precisely because they are divine; that is, because the testimony of the apostles is actually the testimony of the Lord, the exalted Logos, who speaks through them. In this manner the *witness* of the apostles is very much concerned with revelation.

It must also be emphasized, however, that the witness of the apostles is unique. This has already been indicated by the particular position ascribed to them in John 17, by the theme of their commission and by the special impartation to them of Christ's spirit. It is also affirmed by Christ in the promise of the Spirit who will guide them into *all* the truth (16:13). This does not mean that each individual apostle will himself possess all of the truth concerning Jesus. Each will possess only the truth which is revealed to him by Christ. But all of their recollections sanctified by the Spirit of Christ will go together to make up the complete and normative tradition. Cullmann has recognized this truth most clearly in his excellent study of "The Tradition." "Since everything has not been revealed to each individual apostle, each one must first pass on his testimony to another (Gal. 1:18; I Cor. 15:11), and only the entire *paradosis* to which all the apostles contribute, constitutes the *paradosis* of Christ." [13]

This does not mean that the apostles' experience has no analogy in the experience of other Christian men. All men may be said to receive revelation in so far as they believe and understand the

Christian Gospel. But the Gospel is defined by the Lord Himself operating in the apostles. And the Spirit which guides the apostles in the interpretation and preservation of the tradition will only operate upon the minds of other men to lead them to belief in so far as they are met by that same Spirit in a study of their words. The experience of other men is analogous to but does not duplicate the experience of the apostles, not even in the case of their authorized successors. The witness of these men and only their witness can be normative for the faith and the doctrine of the Church.

Finally, as Cullmann goes on to add, the function of the apostle in the New Testament sense can be fulfilled for us only through the Scriptures by which the revelation given through the apostles is preserved. "The apostle cannot, therefore, have any sucessor who can replace him as bearer of the revelation for future generations, but he must continue *himself* to fulfill his function in the Church of today: *in* the Church, not *by* the Church, but *by his word, dia ton logos* (John 17:20), in other words, by his *writings*." [14] Through their writings the apostles continue to speak, and in their testimony the exalted Logos is eternally present in the Church. "These [things] are written that you may believe" (20:31). "This is the disciple . . . who has written these things" (21:24). The significance of this unique testimony, which in the ultimate analysis is to be identified with the New Testament Scriptures, is to be preserved in opposition to the Catholic dogma of a channel of independent revelation through ecclesiastical tradition and against the theory of those Protestants who affirm that the apostolic experience is identical with the deepest religious experience of all believing men. In John's view the New Testament is to take its place along with the Old Testament and the apostles are to take their place along with the prophets as together constituting a unique revelation which is in fact one organic revelation, mediated at all times by the heavenly Christ, the Logos, and centered in Himself as He is revealed to men in the days of His earthly incarnation.

WHO WROTE THE FOURTH GOSPEL?

In carrying the subject of apostolic authorship to the theme of the apostolic writings the question immediately arises as to the authorship of the Fourth Gospel. Can the views just presented be maintained if, as many scholars hold, the Johannine

authorship of the gospel is to be denied? Or is there an incon-
sistency between the gospel's understanding of the apostolic testimony and the supposed fact that the gospel itself is written late
in the first century by a non-apostolic hand? These questions
assume added importance for the present study, not only through
their reference to the apostolic testimony but because the two
texts which have always been taken as affirming most explicitly
the author of the gospel to be the apostle John both employ the
witness terminology. The texts in question are 19:35 and 21:24.

1. The first of these texts (19:35) is in the nature of a verification of the events which took place at the crucifixion and which
are narrated in verses 31 through 34. John says of these events,
"He who saw it has borne witness—his testimony is true, and he
[literally, "that one"] knows that he tells the truth—that you also
may believe." Critical debate on this verse has correctly centered
upon the identity of "the one who saw" these things and upon
the identity of "that one" who knows that he tells the truth.

Today, scholarship is in general agreement on the identity of
the one who saw, nor would there ever have been disagreement
had earlier scholars not at one time been seeking arguments to
deny that the apostle John was the author of the gospel. The
one who saw these things is the "beloved disciple" who alone
of all the disciples is mentioned as being present at the cross
(19:26). This is the disciple mentioned on numerous occasions
throughout the Passion narrative (13:23; 20:2; 21:7, 20) and
is quite possibly also the unnamed disciple who secured Peter's
admission to the court of the high priest during Christ's trial
(18:15, 16). In chapter nineteen the reference is directly parallel
to the case in chapter twenty-one, in which "the disciple who is
bearing witness to these things" is explicitly identified with the
beloved disciple mentioned earlier (verses 7 and 20). There is
no reason to reject the further conclusion that this same disciple
is also the apostle John; for on two occasions at least the beloved
disciple must be identified as one of the twelve (in the account
of the Paschal meal and in the epilogue of chapter twenty-one),
and his close association with Peter (13:24; 20:2; 21:7) as well
as the fact that the apostle John is unmentioned by name any-
where in the gospel more than suggests the identification.

The object of the demonstrative pronoun ("that one") is less
certain and has occasioned more numerous explanations. A num-

ber of scholars, represented in the first instance by Erasmus and at the present time by Strathmann and Bultmann, hold that the reference is to the exalted Christ and interpret the verse as claiming Christ's support for the witness of the beloved disciple. This interpretation accords well with the emphasis upon Christ's witness throughout the gospel and has in its favor the fact that the demonstrative pronoun is elsewhere used of Christ (9:37; I John 3:5, 16), of God (1:33; 5:19, 37; 6:29; 8:42) or of the Holy Spirit (14:26; 15:26; 16:13, 14). But this is very unlike John's handling of the witness terminology. Although he dwells at length upon Christ's witness, he never cites that witness in support of any fact or in support of any person.

Christ's witness is exclusively concerned with revelation, and all other witness points to Him. It is to be added to this observation that although the pronoun is often used of deity, as in the cases cited above, it is never used of deity exclusively and may equally refer, as Bernard notes, to John the Baptist (5:35), Moses (5:46), the man born blind (9:11), Mary of Bethany (11:29), Mary Magdalene (20:15, 16), Peter (18:17, 25) or even, which is much to the point, to the beloved disciple himself (13:25; 21:7, 23). What John's use of the demonstrative does indicate is that the one so designated is "a being who *exclusively* possesses a certain character . . . a *single* person in contrast with *every* other." [15] And as such, the witness may refer equally well to the beloved disciple and/or the author of the gospel.

Some scholars think of "that one" as the author of the gospel considered to be a person other than the witness, according to which the author refers to himself in the third person in order to express his confidence in the witness' testimony. Bernard alludes to this interpretation, noting that it finds support in a similar reference by Josephus to himself in the account of his own activities at Jotapata during the Jewish rebellion of A.D. 66-70 (*The Jewish War,* III, vii, 16).[16] That such a use of the demonstrative occurs in Greek is evident, as other references could also verify, but this view seems controverted by the grammatical construction of the text in which the demonstrative resumes *auton* ("his"), the witness.

The third and at the same time the best identification of the pronoun is with the beloved disciple, a position which seems to be required by the simplest and most literal understanding of the verse. If the demonstrative pronoun does resume *auton,* then the verse must indicate that the witness of the crucifixion is the beloved disciple and that the author of the gospel affirms that he (the beloved disciple) knows that he speaks the truth. It cannot be objected to this interpretation that to refer both of the statements to the witness is redundant, for in the first instance the testimony is described as genuine (*alēthinos*), that is, the proper testimony of an eyewitness, and in the second instance it is also described as being true (*alēthēs*). Both of these conditions are important, and both are met by the witness of the beloved disciple.

To identify both "the one who saw" and "the one who knows that he speaks the truth" with the beloved disciple does not exclude the possibility that this one is also the author of the gospel. For although it is unlikely that the pronoun would designate the author if the author is a person other than the witness, this objection does not hold if the author is the witness; for in this case there is no strain upon the grammatical construction and the verse contains no more than a twofold indirect allusion of the author to himself. Moreover, such an allusion does not seem out of place in view of the other enigmatic references to an unnamed disciple in the gospel. The question at this juncture is, therefore, no longer the antecedents of "the one who saw" and "that one" but whether in both cases the author alludes to a third person, presumably the apostle John from whom he must be distinguished, or to himself as the witness and, therefore, as John, the son of Zebedee.

Following Westcott's excellent analysis three points call for special notice. First, there is every reason why in this context the evidence of the evangelist should be appealed to in the third person and as an item of historical veracity. The evangelist has already been presented as an historical figure present at the crucifixion, and there is every reason why the evangelist should now draw attention to himself in this capacity, as a witness to the events described. If this is the Johannine concern, one must reckon with the possibility that the solemnity of John's affirmation in this verse may be due, not primarily to the supposed mystical or sacramental significance of the events described, although it no doubt includes it, but to the fact that he can produce only one witness, that is, only one apostle as a witness, the beloved disciple, whose witness nevertheless is true.

Second, the testimony involved is spoken of as something which has been given and which abides with present significance. The author uses the perfect tense of the testimony—"He who saw it has borne witness"—and uses the present tense of the witness' understanding of his words—"He knows that he is telling the truth." The natural implication of these tenses is that the witness was still living at the time of the writing of the gospel and that the present testimony to which allusion is made is contained in the substance of the gospel.

Finally, if the witness were a third person to whose testimony John appeals, the evangelist would more naturally have used an aorist tense than a perfect tense as is the case. The conclusion seems to be that if the alternative above may be accepted—that in both references the evangelist refers either to himself or to a third person as the witness—the natural reading of the passage tends to identify the evangelist with the witness and, therefore, to identify both with John, the son of Zebedee. This conclusion carries such weight that Macgregor, who denies that "that one" is the evangelist and who affirms he is the witness, nevertheless makes the admission that the verse is most likely the addition of a Redactor "in which the point of view of the Appendix is thrown back into the body of the Gospel in order to suggest that the Witness-Evangelist (according to the Redactor they are one person) is to be identified with the Beloved Disciple." [17]

An added indication of the probability of this conclusion is to be found in the fact that appeal is made to this eyewitness in order that "you also may believe." This verse becomes by the precise expression of this purpose an exact parallel to John 20: 30, 31 in which the eyewitness of the disciples and the writing of their reminiscences is particularly directed toward the belief of those who read the gospel. Granted John's recognition of the role of the apostle as the verifier of the tradition and the certain reference to that function in 20:30, 31, it is practically certain that the evangelist indicates an apostle and not merely an unnamed and otherwise unknown disciple in 19:35. As an apostle the witness who saw these things bears witness, not only to the surprising issue of water and blood from the side of the expired Lord, but to the entire scene, all of the events of which occurred in fulfillment of the Scriptures (verses 36 and 37).

2. The second text which has generally been understood to

affirm the Johannine authorship of the gospel is 21:24, the first half of the postscript which concludes the appendix to the gospel (chapter 21). This verse asserts in reference to the preceding events, "This is the disciple who is bearing witness to these things, and who has written these things; and we know that his testimony is true." Since the opening pronoun can only refer to the beloved disciple mentioned in the immediately preceding narrative (verses 7 and 20), historically this verse has always been understood to identify the author of the gospel with the beloved disciple and, hence, with the apostle John.

In the light of the themes under consideration in this chapter, several aspects of this verse call for special notice. In the first place, it is not only said that the beloved disciple is the witness who rendered testimony to the events that are recorded in the gospel, but also that the disciple wrote them down. Here certainly is the strongest possible evidence for affirming that the beloved disciple stood behind the greatest part if not the entire composition of the gospel.

The second point of special interest is the antecedent of "these things." This word may refer either to the whole of the gospel including chapter twenty-one, to chapters one through twenty (that is, to the gospel minus the appendix), or to chapter twenty-one alone. If chapter twenty-one together with the concluding verses was a separate composition, as some have maintained, then the "these things" of verse 24 refers exclusively to it. There is no reason to believe that this was ever the case, however, nor even, if the chapter was of separate origin, to think that the closing remarks were composed before it was added to the gospel. The appendix is not of such importance that it would merit such a closing, and the verses in question have the character of a final authorization of the gospel. Whether the ascription of verse 24 refers to the entire gospel including the appendix or to the proper body of the gospel without it is a problem which is harder to resolve. As it stands the verse naturally refers to all that precedes it, including especially the story of Christ's words in regard to the beloved disciple. But to those who deny that the closing chapter is by the same hand as the hand which wrote the gospel or to those who maintain that the author of verse 24 must be identical with the author of the appendix, "these things" must refer to the gospel without the appendix. In either case the apostle John is claimed, not only as the witness, but also as the author of the gospel properly so called.

The question of the claim of authorship, which is the primary concern in this section, is already decided by these considerations, but there exists the further and quite interesting question as to the author to whom these closing words should be assigned. It is conceivable, of course, that the words could be from the author of the gospel. But this is highly improbable and has been assumed to be improbable above. If one is to believe that the author himself composed these verses, it becomes impossible to explain the express identification of himself as the beloved disciple, for up to this point the evangelist has been careful to remain anonymous. Moreover, the first person plural of the final phrase of verse 24 ("and *we* know that his testimony is true") seems different from John's own way of referring to himself as indicated in 19:35. These considerations suggest that the "we" of 21:24 is to be understood as representing some official body capable of identifying the author with the beloved disciple, an eyewitness of many if not all of the events described, and of attesting his character and the inherent reliability of his testimony.[18]

If this is true, then the evidence of the gospel to its own authorship is twofold: first by the author himself in reference to the witness of the crucifixion which occurs in 19:35, and second by the leaders of his church who add an express identification of the author with John.

It should be added, of course, that the denial of a reference to the apostles as eyewitnesses in 21:24 does not also imply a denial of that reference in all instances in which the gospel speaks of "we." Although the plural of 21:24 presumably denotes the witness of the Church, the identification of the "we" with the Church authorities need not inveigh against the identification of other plural forms, composed by the author of the gospel himself, with the witness and authority of the apostolate.

One such case has already been discussed in chapter three, the reference on Christ's lips to those who "speak of what we know, and bear witness to what we have seen" in 3:11. This witness is presumably that of the apostolic band considered together with Jesus, the disciples bearing witness, not through any perception of their own, but as those who have heard and seen what Christ has made known to them. To this instance may be added the case of 1:14: "We have beheld his glory, glory as of the only Son from the Father." The natural meaning of this verse is that the fourth evangelist claims at the beginning of the gospel to be an eyewitness of the events he is about to narrate. To deny an eyewitness report in this context is to reject the entire purpose of the passage which teaches that the incarnation was historical and that Jesus as an historical personage was observed by many. It is impossible to consider this text without at the same time calling attention to the claim for eyewitness authority on the part of the apostles at 15:27 and to the quite similar claim to have seen, looked upon and touched the incarnate Lord in I John 1:1-4.

These passages, taken together with the more explicit claims of 19:35 and 21:24, constitute an internal and nearly unquestionable claim on the part of the writer of the gospel and of those who authenticate his work that the gospel is the account of an eyewitness who had been with Jesus from the beginning, who was the only disciple to have witnessed the crucifixion, and that this disciple was none other than the beloved disciple who was the apostle John.

A NEW LOOK IN JOHANNINE STUDIES

It must be acknowledged at this point, however, that discussion of the authorship of the Fourth Gospel in contemporary studies goes far beyond the internal evidence of the gospel itself to its origin and that the explicit statements of 19:35 and 21:24 do not always play an important role in these discussions. For the present study a discussion of these texts was imperative; first because they each contain an example of the witness terminology and, second, because it is the gospel itself which is under consideration and not current theories as to its authorship. At the same time the question remains: Can the gospel's claim to eyewitness support and authorship together with its acknowledgment of the role of the apostles as the normative bearers of the apostolic tradition be seriously regarded if at the same time the student is compelled by critical scholarship to reject the apostolic origin either of the gospel itself or of the tradition which lies immediately behind it?

If Johannine authorship in any form is rigidly rejected, does this not inevitably militate against the importance of the apostolic witness and, thus, ultimately against the entire concept of eye-witness testimony as that theme is developed in the gospel? It is the conviction of the present writer that this is so—that the evangelist's doctrine of the apostolate must be borne out in the practical composition of the gospel—but that a total rejection of apostolic authorship is no longer required by critical scholarship and is in fact increasingly coming under attack as an inadequate explanation of the gospel and its origins.

The so-called shift in scholarship has been pointed up by a number of authors, among them Cullmann, who speaks of "a new approach" to the interpretation of the Fourth Gospel, and J. A. T. Robinson, who writes of the "new look" in Johannine studies.[19] Comparing contemporary approaches to John's gospel with the critical orthodoxy of the first half of the twentieth century, these scholars detect a tendency today to perceive a genuinely historical and even apostolic tradition in the Fourth Gospel and even to go so far as to recognize the evangelist (although perhaps not the author of the gospel as it now stands) as a contemporary of Jesus Christ and an eyewitness of the events described. At least five factors have contributed to this new approach:

1. Increased knowledge of the New Testament period has led to general acknowledgment of the existence of a non-conformist Judaism in Palestine before the Christian era, a Judaism embracing genuine Hellenistic tendencies not far removed from the supposedly Greek elements that have always been noted in the Fourth Gospel. This increased knowledge is due in large measure to the discovery of the Dead Sea Scrolls in 1947 and their publication in subsequent years. In particular, there is a growing readiness to recognize that the life and the literature of the Qumran community may represent the historical milieu out of which John the Baptist emerged with his message of repentance and baptism and also the historical background of the author of the gospel.

An excellent illustration is to be found in the so-called Gnosticism of the Fourth Gospel, upon which much Johannine scholarship is built. This has often been considered a product of Hellenistic Christianity. Today it is increasingly recognized that the closest parallels to these Johannine themes are found, not in the thought of Asia Minor, but in what Reicke calls the "pre-Gnostic" thought forms of the Qumran community.[20] A. M. Hunter writes, listing K. G. Kuhn, Albright, Burrows, W. H. Brownlee, Jeremias, and Reicke for support, "The dualism which pervades the Johannine writings is of precisely the same kind as we discover in the Dead Sea Scrolls; not physical or substantial (as in the Greek Gnostics) but monotheistic, ethical, eschatological." [21] It is also to be noted that other themes apparently Hellenistic (the Logos, life and light) are essentially the products of Jewish modes of thought.

This argument asserts, not that the fourth evangelist himself emerged from the environment of Qumran—few would argue this —but that the Dead Sea Scrolls provide tangible evidence for the existence in Palestine, even in the southern and most Jewish sectors of the country, of a body of ideas perfectly adequate to account for the distinctive beliefs and thought forms evident in the gospel. Robinson, assessing the historical background, says:

> I detect a growing readiness to recognize that this is not to be sought at the end of the first century or the beginning of the second, in Ephesus or Alexandria, among the Gnostics or the Greeks. Rather, there is no compelling need to let our gaze wander very far, either in space or in time, beyond a fairly limited area of southern Palestine in the fairly limited interval between the crucifixion and the fall of Jerusalem.

He adds that the Dead Sea Scrolls "may really represent an actual background, and not merely a possible environment, for the distinctive categories of the gospel." [22]

2. The reliability of the Johannine topography, vindicated by archaeological discovery, also points in its own way to the author's familiarity with southern Palestine and to the historical trustworthiness of the narrative. The evangelist mentions several places known to the Synoptic writers that might therefore be known generally through tradition: Bethsaida (1:44; 12:21), the Praetorium (18:28, 33; 19:9), and Bethany (11:18). But he also speaks accurately of Ephraim (11:54), Sychar, which is probably to be identified with Shechem at Tell Balatah (4:5), Solomon's Porch (10:23), the brook Kidron, which Jesus crossed to reach Gethsemane (18:1), and Bethany beyond Jordan, which he distinguishes from the other Bethany only fifteen furlongs from Jerusalem (1:28). In recent years the reliability of the writer's knowledge of Jerusalem has received additional verification by

the discovery of an old reservoir with five porticoes near the sheep gate, undoubtedly corresponding to the Pool of Bethesda (5:2), and by identification of the Pavement of judgment, *Gabbatha* (19:13), as an area in the northwest corner of the temple enclosure bordering on the tower of Antonia.

The most striking of the archaeological discoveries is the probable identification of Aenon near Salim, where there were "many waters" (3:23), with Ainun ("little fountain"), lying near the head waters of the Wadi Farah. The author's accurate reference to such an obscure site indicates a remarkable familiarity with the area of the Jordan, and the general knowledge of Jerusalem and its environments which he displays argues strongly that his information about Palestine was firsthand.

3. Of equal importance with the increased knowledge of the conditions in Palestine during the Christian era is a greater sensitivity to the uniqueness in content of the Fourth Gospel, brought to light by an intensified comparison with the Synoptic narratives.

At one time the very uniqueness of the final gospel would have been taken as an argument for its historical unreliability and as a sign of the distance in time between its composition and the events it describes. Today this is no longer so. With the shift in interest in New Testament studies generally from specific problems of authorship to the gospel traditions that the individual compositions represent, there has come a new awareness of the potential reliability of any independent testimony and a willingness to accept the unique Johannine traditions as being at least as old as the traditions represented by the Synoptics. Many scholars today regard the case for a literary dependence of John on the Synoptics as unproven and improbable. Some even consider the possibility of a dependence of the Synoptics upon John. The weightiest work in English to advance the case for literary independence is the exhaustive examination of *Historical Tradition in the Fourth Gospel* by C. H. Dodd. Although Dodd prefers to leave the question of authorship in abeyance, his whole work is designed to show that "behind the Fourth Gospel lies an ancient tradition independent of the other gospels, and meriting serious consideration as a contribution to our knowledge of the historical facts concerning Jesus Christ." [23]

In this area of Johannine studies, few dismiss the theological nature or even the original character of John's work; but many

now regard his teaching to be at least as old as the Pauline theology and, in terms of the tradition, as historically reliable as the
Synoptic gospels on those points where it is to be taken as history.

It should be added that if this line of study is in error—if the
Johannine traditions are not entirely independent of the Synoptics
and the gospel itself makes use of Mark or Luke—then even in
this case, owing to John's intentional variation upon the Synoptic
accounts, the argument for an eyewitness tradition merits equally
serious consideration. Streeter, who considers John the Presbyter
to be the author of the gospel, makes this reasoning plain:

> The more the difference between the theological standpoint
> of John and the Synoptics is stressed, the more inexplicable
> becomes John's policy of contradicting them on details of his-
> tory on which doctrinally nothing turns. . . . But if the author
> of the Fourth Gospel had himself visited Jerusalem . . .
> he might consider himself to be in a position to correct or
> explain, as one having authority, the story as told in these
> two gospels [Mark and Luke]. While the difficulty of ex-
> plaining his boldness in so drastically correcting the lives of
> Christ hitherto known in the Church for which he wrote
> would disappear completely, if we could suppose that he
> could claim in any sense to be himself an eye-witness.[24]

4. The new recognition of the possibility of John's authorship of the Fourth Gospel or of a genuine eyewitness experience
as a basis of the traditions it incorporates has been given added
stimulus by the attempt to find within the gospel traces of Aramaic
idiom or of original Aramaic documents that are supposed to
underlie it. This area of research has been controversial. But
though the case of Burney and Torrey for an Aramaic original
of the Fourth Gospel (in Torrey's case of all four gospels) has
hardly met with general acceptance, it seems quite probable,
nonetheless, that a strong Semitic idiom does underlie part of the
Fourth Gospel, if not the whole. This may be indicative of a
Hebrew- or Aramaic-speaking author who composed his narrative in Greek. Dodd observes that "the evidence for an underlying Semitic idiom is irresistible" and that "this in itself brings
the Gospel back into a Jewish environment, of which we must
take account." [25]

In itself this factor may not prove the existence of an Aramaic-
speaking author, but it does make it difficult to associate the

gospel solely with Hellenistic thought-currents or to locate its historical background exclusively in Asia Minor and see it as a representation of Greek-speaking Christianity. Taken together with the other items mentioned, this factor substantially increases the probability that the witness who stands behind the gospel and to whom must be attributed a share of the actual composition, if not the authorship of the whole, was a Jew of Palestine and thus a possible eyewitness of the events of Christ's ministry.

5. The final factor that has weighed heavily in an assessment of the Johannine authorship of the gospel is the belated discovery by critical scholars that the so-called theological (Clement calls it a "spiritual") interest of the gospel does not militate against an equally serious attention to the facts.

Not many would doubt today that John is concerned with what has been called for lack of a better term "the Christ of faith." He affirms indeed that "the flesh is of no avail" (6:63) and asserts repeatedly, as in the account of the post-resurrection appearance to Thomas, that belief must take precedence over sight. But for John the Christ of faith includes the Jesus of history, and belief, though it represents a step beyond the evidence, nevertheless is based upon it. In fact, as Robinson believes, the notion that the Christ of faith can be had apart from the Jesus of history is "exactly the error which, to judge from the prologue and the epistles, he was most concerned to combat." [26] A recognition of these facts has led some scholars to speak of a twofold concern in John's approach to history, a concern, as Cullmann expresses it, for "faith in the Jesus of history as the 'Christ.'" [27] Or as Hoskyns writes, "The visible, historical Jesus is the place in history where it is demanded that men should believe." [28] If these two interests are really interwoven, then it is hard to see how the spiritual interests could be maintained without an equally serious attention to the history and how the historical interest could be genuine without an equal concern for verified historical material. It is contributory to this line of thought that John places an exceptional importance on the facts and in particular upon verification of the facts by those who witnessed them.

It would be unwarranted, of course, to suggest that the question of the authorship of the Fourth Gospel is now receiving an answer radically different from that given by scholars a decade or two ago. Because of the opening up of these new interests, the question of authorship has actually assumed a much less important place and has received much less direct discussion. At the same time, however, it is warranted to speak of a new look in Johannine studies according to which scholars more readily admit the possibility of apostolic authorship and speak even more surely of a primitive and reliable tradition underlying the historical material of the gospel. There appears to be no conclusive reason why this tradition may not be, as the gospel itself declares it to be, the eyewitness tradition of a contemporary of the Lord. If this is so, then the role of the apostolic witness is vindicated in the composition of the gospel. If it is not, there is still every ground for acknowledging the role of the apostles or of an individual apostle as the source, guardian and authority behind the traditions which are embodied in the text. And this is to acknowledge the apostles, not only as eyewitnesses, but as those inspired interpreters of the tradition through whom the risen Lord has continued to testify and in whose written reminiscences that testimony, the mediated testimony of the Lord, remains active and ever present in the Church.

THE TESTIMONY OF OTHER HUMAN WITNESSES

There are also a number of other witnesses included by the evangelist which justify an extension of the subject of human witness from the exceptional witness of the apostles to the theme of human witness in general, including the testimony of all men to Christ in all ages of the Christian Church. The woman of Samaria is one such witness. The multitude which witnesses the resurrection of Lazarus is another. Moreover, although John does not use the word witness in chapter nine, the man who had been born blind also emerges strongly in this role. These examples indicate that John's use of the witness terminology extends beyond the supernatural testimony of Jesus, the prophets, and the apostles to include the experience of all believers. And this extension stimulates thought about the meaning of a purely human witness.

The first pertinent observation upon the examples of human witness just cited is that in every case human witness has the characteristics of a *response* to the divine revelation, a response to the external revelation given in the events of Christ's life and ministry and a response to the internal revelation of the meaning of those events given by the operation of the divine Spirit upon the mind of the observer. In both the initiative is unquestionably with God.

This is quite clear of the external revelation. There can be no testimony to what Christ has done until He has done it. There can be no response to His words until He speaks them. This is of primary importance. It is a clear indication of the nature of witness as a response to the external revelation that Christ Himself is the object of the witness and not the experience of the believer, however it may be conceived. Externally, as has been noted many times already, the revelation is focused exclusively in Christ, involving His life, death, and resurrection together with all His actions and all His teachings. And hence, if the human witness is really a response to the revelation, it must be of necessity a response to that which is revealed in Christ, to Christ Himself; and Christ Himself must be the object of the witness. This is precisely the teaching of the fourth evangelist. The multitude which witnesses the raising of Lazarus from the dead testifies, not to their presence at the tomb, although that presence is a presupposition of their witness bearing, but to Jesus who "called Lazarus out of the tomb and raised him from the dead" (12:17). The man who had been born blind does not testify to the fact that *he* was healed, although his personal experience is what constituted him a witness, but to the one who "opened the eyes of a man born blind" (9:32). The woman of Samaria calls attention to Jesus in His prophetic capacity. "He told me all that I ever did" (4:39). Similarly, John the Baptist, the Twelve, and the eyewitness of the passion bear witness to Jesus Himself exclusively or to a specific aspect of His death or ministry.

That the object of human testimony is Jesus Christ and not the experience of the observer does not mean, of course, that there is no significance to the personal experience of the individual. On the contrary, it is precisely because of the personal observation, as in the case of the disciples (later apostles) who were with Christ from the beginning, that the witness to Christ Himself is possible. Human testimony is made in response to the facts which each individual can verify. The woman of Samaria does not testify of Christ's ability to do miracles, nor does the man who was born blind witness to Christ's knowledge of his past life. Each testifies to Christ only in reference to that which he or she experienced. And the testimony is all the more impressive for that fact. In every case, however, the object of the witness is not the experience but the one recognized in the experience, to whom, and to whom personally, a response is made in faith. Because the witness of God is made *in Christ,* that is, in an historical event, the witness of Christians today becomes in its turn, not a conceptual reasoning or rational arguing about a philosophical God, but a pointing back to Christ, as the place and moment when the truth was manifested and the light was allowed to shine forth in the darkness of this world. Barth writes that "a true witness of God does not proceed as an original witness; he looks back to the witnesses of God who were before him and takes up their testimony as God's testimony." He is an "expositor, an explainer, an interpreter." [29] The human witness responds to and declares belief in that which has already been revealed. It is the revelation demanding and obtaining a response which makes a man a witness.

It is equally apparent, however, that the witness of the believer must be more than a response to the external revelation given in the events and teachings of Christ's ministry. It must also be a response to an internal revelation, to the operation of God's Spirit upon the human mind in such a manner that the truth of Christ's claims and His identity as the Son of God are made a living reality for the individual in confrontation with the facts concerning Him. Here again the initiative is with God who gives the revelation; human response, which is faith, is secondary.

John uses a number of terms to express the reality of his response to the internal revelation. He speaks of "receiving the testimony" (3:11, 32, 33), of "hearing" with spiritual understanding (6:45; 8:47; 9:27), of "seeing" what has been revealed (1:34; 3:11, 32), of "knowing" in a sense which implies a spiritual perception, and of "believing" which is the Johannine equivalent of faith. In each case the verb indicates a believing response to the revelation on the part of the individual and places the initiative in such an encounter with God.

The same truth is evident in another way in respect to some of the gospel's remarks about the truth. In 18:37, just after He has described the purpose of His incarnation as a coming to bear witness to the truth, Jesus further adds that "every one who is of the truth hears my voice" (cf. also 3:21). And in 4:23, 24, Jesus declares that true worshipers must worship the Father "in spirit and truth." In these instances Jesus can only mean that the capacity of an individual to receive the revelation is preceded and is in fact made possible by the work of the Father in implanting the divine reality within his heart. The background of the Johannine statements lies in the teaching that the election and supernatural activity of God preceded the human response, creating the faith, and that it is the reception of revelation so revealed which makes a man a witness. In some instances, as in Jesus' admonition to the Jews in 8:32, "truth" becomes the object of "knowledge," and true knowledge emerges as the perception and reception of the truth by those who are characterized by it.

Quite clearly the internal response of the individual may not be separated from the external revelation, for the internal perception is a perception of the meaning of the facts. This is evident, on the one hand, from the function of the signs. Miracles are not the results of faith; they are manifestations of the glory of God, and they provoke faith on the part of the beholder. Thus, the external revelation of the power of Jesus over death is the effective cause of faith on the part of the multitude in chapters eleven and twelve. The revelation of Jesus in His prophetic character and in His ability to heal the sick produces believing witnesses in the persons of the woman of Samaria and the man who had been born blind. The previous revelation to John the Baptist together with the external sign given at the baptism enable the forerunner to designate Jesus as the pre-existent, sin-bearing Lamb of God. And the ability of the disciples to testify to the actual events of Jesus' ministry becomes the formal pre-condition of their apostleship.

It is to be noticed also that the stories of the encounter of individuals with Jesus in the gospel seldom terminate with the incident itself but pass on almost inevitably to some form of Christological confession. The man born blind is last seen in an attitude of worship voicing the confession, "Lord, I believe" (9:38). In the narrative of the woman of Samaria one perceives a growth in the woman's understanding of the Lord. At the beginning of the conversation Jesus is only regarded as a Jew (4:9). In verse 12 the woman voices the possibility that He may be greater than the patriarch Jacob. In verse 19 He is called a prophet. And the conclusion comes in the testimony to her neighbors when the woman suggests that Jesus may be the Messiah (4:29).

A recognition of the close connection between an external response to the facts and an internal response in faith is further encouraged by reflection upon the opening series of testimonies in chapter one where Jesus is called Messiah by Andrew, the fulfiller of the law and the prophets by Philip, the Son of God and King of Israel by Nathanael, and by the incidents later in the gospel in which Jesus is termed the Savior of the world (4:42), the prophet (6:14; 9:17), the Holy One of God (6:69) and many times simply the Christ, the Messiah (7:41; 11:27). The gospel reaches its climax in the very personal confession of Thomas, "My Lord and my God!" (20:28). The goal of all personal experience is this believing testimony. In this response to revelation the external and the internal response go hand in hand. Experience is present, but in every instance the object of the witness is not the telling of the experience but the pointing to Jesus who is perceived in faith. This is the Christological confession.[30]

Human witness is not only a response, however, for response could be restricted to the past and could be localized within the mind of the believer. Human witness is also a vocalized confession and must have a reference to the present. It is a task, a ministry. And this is to say that human witness has as its second characteristic the fact that it is *mission*. In acknowledging this characteristic the fourth evangelist acknowledges the active side of witness and places a demand upon his readers which was equally acknowledged of the prophets (Neh. 9:26), of the Psalmist (Psalm 40:9, 10), and even of the people of Israel in general under the Old Testament dispensation (Isaiah 43:8-13; 44:6-8). There can be no true confession without a prior response to the revelation in faith, but similarly there can be no real faith without an inevitable expression of that faith in witness. Michel has perceived this truth clearly in an article on the biblical idea of witness and confession, noting at one point that the biblical faith cannot live without confession as a function of that faith.[31] In biblical thought the obligation to testify is vital to the faith and is inseparably connected with the response of the individual to grace.

John says the same thing in a number of ways. In 12:43 he indicates his disapproval of secret discipleship, presumably practiced by a man like Nicodemus (cf. 7:50-52), indicating that some of the rulers believed on Jesus yet did not confess Him. "For they loved the praise of men more than the praise of God." In several instances he speaks of "receiving the witness," a phrase

which is unique to John (3:11, 33; 5:34; I John 5:9; cf. John
12:48; 17:8). John means that human witness is a task; revelation is a thing to be shared. The same type of thought occurs
three times in the book of Revelation in the phrase "to have the
testimony" (Rev. 6:9; 12:17; 19:10). The subject in every instance is believers. Finally, John also speaks of the obligation
to "confess" Jesus. One instance is found in the warning against
secret discipleship already cited (12:42, 43) where the reference
is to a vocalized acknowledgment of that which has already been
believed. The same is true in the case of John the Baptist who
"confessed, he did not deny, but confessed, 'I am not the Christ'"
(1:20). Similarly, John notes that the Jewish rulers decided to
expel from the synagogue any who should make open confession
that Jesus is the Christ (9:22). In the light of the experience
of the Christian Church in the first generation of its existence it
would seem that John's concern for a vocalized testimony to
Jesus on the part of all believers arises not merely from the Old
Testament demand which it reflects but also from the necessity
of the early Christian community to carry its message of salvation and revelation in Jesus to the Jewish, Greek, and Roman
worlds. The success or failure of early Christianity depended in
no small measure upon such vocalized confessions.

For a believer to witness in the Johannine sense is, however,
not merely to provide authenticating statements of what he has
seen and heard but also by his life and conduct to be the instrument through which the object of the witness, Jesus Christ Himself, is made known to the unbelieving world. This theme emerges
strikingly in the final discourses in reference to what the Lord
expects of His disciples. They are to be one among themselves,
just as Jesus and the Father are one (14:20; 17:11, 21, 22), that
"the world may know that thou hast sent me and hast loved
them even as thou hast loved me" (17:23). They are to be
consecrated to their task "in truth" (17:19). And John adds
that believers are to do the truth (3:21; I John 1:6, 7) as well
as to learn and teach it. At every point the reality of the revelation which has come in Christ is to be reproduced in the life of
the believer. Their witness is to involve Christ's ethic, and this
will be produced in them by the power of the Spirit which is
active in Scripture. They are to combine a word and a deed witness in their testimony just as a word and a deed witness are

organically united in His own. They are to be His representatives, living monuments in which Christ's glory may be seen.

All of these statements converge in saying that the subject of human witness, by deeds as well as by words, ends finally with the necessity for mission, with the need to carry the Gospel once revealed in Jesus and defined by the apostles to every people, every tongue, and every nation, the Gospel of the One who was lifted up that He might draw all men unto Himself. To bear witness is the task of the disciple. It only remains to show that in the performance of this mission as well as in its inception, the human witness to Jesus depends upon and is made possible by the operation of the divine Spirit upon the minds of men.

Chapter 6

The Witness of the Holy Spirit

Ever since the publication of Luther's *Small Catechism* in 1529, the publication of the expanded *Institutes of the Christian Religion* thirty years later, and the appearance in those years of several other less influential Reformation volumes, the idea of the witness of the Spirit in the Fourth Gospel has been central to that doctrine which reformed theologians have called the *internal* witness of the Holy Spirit (*testimonium Spiritus Sancti internum*). By this phrase is meant the supernatural and saving activity of the Holy Spirit on behalf of the one who hears the Gospel so that the reality of what is taught is conveyed to the mind, producing the conviction that this is truth and leading the soul to receive it to its consequent salvation. Luther taught that the Holy Spirit "calls, gathers, enlightens, and sanctifies the whole Christian Church on earth." And Calvin added that "the Word will not find acceptance in men's hearts before it is sealed by the inward testimony of the Spirit. . . . Without the illumination of the Holy Spirit, the Word can do nothing."[1] Because the reformed doctrine of the Holy Spirit has always been based in a large measure upon the teachings of the Fourth Gospel, it is in reference to this doctrine that John's use of the words "witness" and "testimony" has always been most clearly referred to revelation.

A number of texts make this connection clear. In chapter three in conversation with Nicodemus, Jesus speaks of the new birth, noting that it is a product of the activity of the Spirit. "The wind blows where it will, and you hear the sound of it, but you do not know whence it comes or whither it goes; so it is with every one who is born of the Spirit" (3:8). In the final discourses Jesus speaks of the Spirit as one who will dwell in the disciples and who will lead them into all the truth. "He will teach you all things, and bring to your remembrance all that I have said to you" (14:26; cf. 15:26; 16:12-15). In the first epistle John states that "you have been anointed by the Holy One" and "the anointing which you received from him abides in you, and you have no need that any one should teach you" (I John 2:20, 27). "The Spirit is the witness, because the Spirit is the truth" (I John 5:7). The same idea is present in numerous other passages of the New Testament (cf. I Cor. 2:12-15; Eph. 1:16-20). In all of these texts the teaching is that, not only man's rebirth, but his entire growth in spiritual wisdom and in the knowledge of God through Scripture is the result of the working of the divine Spirit upon his life and mind and that no such understanding is possible apart from the Spirit's life-giving activity. The witness of the Holy Spirit is, therefore, the subjective counterpart in revelation of the objective, historical revelation manifested in Christ and recorded in the written Word of God.

The doctrine of the Holy Spirit in John is not without its difficulties, however, and it is to these difficulties that most recent Johannine scholarship has turned. Does the Fourth Gospel represent one or more than one doctrine of the Spirit? When is the Spirit given? And what is the real meaning of Christ's careful allusions to the Paraclete, those enigmatic references to the Spirit which are unique to the Johannine writings?

The problem of the Paraclete arises from the fact that the word itself (*paraklētos*) can be considered either passive or active in form. If it is passive, which is most likely, the word must mean "advocate," literally "one who is called to the side of." And it must have a primary reference to the processes of law. In this sense it is correctly used of Jesus Himself in I John 2:1 in reference to His activity in heaven on behalf of believers, and it is correctly translated as "advocate" in this context by most of the major English versions (cf. Matt. 10:32, 33; Mark 8:38). In the same way it is possible that the Spirit could also be an advocate for the disciples. But in John this function is never explicitly given to the Spirit in relation to His activity on earth, and, as far as the disciples are concerned, the Spirit is more of a teacher than an advocate in a judicial setting. He reveals the things of

Christ. In one sense and in one passage the Paraclete is described as being something like Christ's advocate before the world (16: 8-11); but even here the Paraclete is more of an accuser than a counsel, and this theme is apparently an extension of the other, more basic idea, rather than the root from which the doctrine of the revealing Spirit comes.

On the other hand, if the active meaning of Paraclete is chosen —although this is less acceptable—then the word suggests "one who consoles" or "Comforter." In this case the difficulty lies in reconciling the idea of comfort with the revelational and judgmental aspects of the Spirit's witness.

The solution to this dilemma is either to be sought in a radical reinterpretation of the Johannine teaching, with a consequent reinterpretation of the reformed doctrine, or else in the discovery of an alternate meaning of Paraclete which permits and gives meaning to the statements which are given in the gospel. In contemporary Johannine scholarship both of these channels have been sounded.

Actually, the role of the Spirit in the Fourth Gospel cannot be understood apart from the theological interests of the evangelist, just as the theme of witness cannot be understood apart from those same interests. The problems associated with the original meaning of the Paraclete are technical ones, and these are important. But the determinative questions are those which concern the Spirit's functions in revelation and, more generally, the place which the Johannine doctrine of the Spirit holds in the gospel as a whole. What is the context of the doctrine of the Spirit in John? Theologically, the functions of the Spirit are best understood against the background of the problem of belief, the problem of "seeing and believing" as it is called in recent studies.

SEEING AND BELIEVING

The theme of seeing and believing has come to occupy an increasingly large place in recent discussions of the Johannine theology as many scholars have come to recognize that the gospel manifests a remarkable interest in the connection between the act of belief and the seeing of the object of that belief. John's "seeing and believing" corresponds in some measure to "hearing and believing" in Paul. But in the Pauline letters hearing follows the preaching of the Word (Rom. 10:14-17); in John the parallel is to the seeing of Jesus as He is portrayed in the pages of the gospel.

John begins the gospel with the assertion that the disciples *saw* the glory of Christ in the days of His flesh (1:14), and he ends the gospel proper with a challenge to his readers to believe. "Now Jesus did many other signs in the presence of the disciples, which are not written in this book; but these are written that you may *believe* that Jesus is the Christ, the Son of God, and that *believing* you may have life in his name" (20:30, 31). John uses the verb "believe" nearly one hundred times in the gospel alone, and also places great emphasis upon the literal seeing, feeling, tasting and hearing of Jesus Christ. On several occasions, as in the verse which is presumably John's personal testimony of the moment in which he believed, the ideas of seeing and believing are united. "Then the other disciple, who reached the tomb first, also went in, and he *saw and believed*" (20:8; cf. also 6:40; 12:44-46). Similarly, in 5:24 Jesus speaks of the one "who *hears* my word and *believes* him who sent me." This believing is the Johannine equivalent of faith. (John never uses the noun for faith, except in I John 5:4; he always uses the verb.) And this means that faith itself, the fundamental event of the Christian life, is inseparable from sight.

But what is meant by sight? How are belief and sight related? And how is it that men can see now that Christ has returned to heaven? These questions have unusual significance for an interpretation of the events of the gospel, for, according to the evangelist's own statement in 20:30 and 31, it is for belief that the particular incidents recorded in the gospel have been chosen.

Cullmann more than others has been active in an investigation of these themes, and many of his observations are of help in this connection. In an essay entitled *"Eiden kai episteysen"* for the Maurice Goguel *Festschrift* (1950) and in a discussion of "The Evangelist's Purpose" for the monograph on *Early Christian Worship,* Cullmann rightly rejects all attempts to combine the ideas of seeing and believing into one. Belief is not achieved merely by seeking the support of an eyewitness, however important that may be. Nor is seeing to be understood only as a spiritual seeing and thereby made synonymous with faith.

> The necessity of seeing in the flesh is stressed on the one hand and that of faith on the other hand. In actual fact,

this method of setting two things side by side is characteristic
of all the fourth evangelist's thinking.

In the whole Gospel of John, both aspects, the eyewitness
and the interpretation of faith, are emphasized in their necessary *connection* and in their *distinction*.[2]

The interplay of these two ideas is evident in a number of passages in the gospel to which Cullmann draws attention. In the
account of the resurrection of Lazarus, for instance, John seems
purposely to emphasize the joy of Jesus that He was not present
during the last hours of Lazarus' sickness so that the disciples
might witness this most sublime of miracles. "And for your sake
I am glad that I was not there, so that you may believe" (11:15).
"Taken together with verse 21: ('If you had been here my brother
would not have died'), this can only mean that the disciples
should have the opportunity of *seeing* the miracle of raising the
dead, in order to attain to faith."[3] John then goes on to add
that many who were standing by also believed on Him (11:45).
Seeing and believing are not identical in this incident, for many
see who do not believe. But seeing and believing belong together,
the object of sight being that it might lead a man to faith.

The interplay of faith and sight also figures in the instances
of spiritual insight recorded in the opening chapter of the gospel, incidents which are a commentary upon the pressing invitation
to "Come and see" (1:39, 46), as well as in all the instances in
which a sign is given to lead a man to faith.

So also in the demand of Thomas to touch the risen Lord.
Thomas is not, as Bultmann says, a representation of the bulk
of men who cannot believe without miracles or signs.[4] He demands no more than the other apostles have already received, a
visible manifestation of the risen Christ as evidence of His bodily
resurrection. Thomas must see. As an apostle he must touch
the risen Lord. But physical contact is not and cannot be sufficient even for apostles, and Thomas must go on to an expression of belief. Thomas answers, "My Lord and my God!" (20:
28). It was necessary for the eyewitnesses to see, but even for
them something had to be added to the seeing. They too must
believe. They too must be instructed by the Spirit. Such spiritual
understanding has already been discussed more fully in reference
to the apostolic witness, and it is this which provides the evangelist with his distinctive understanding of the meaning of the

events of Christ's ministry, particularly as these relate to the
sacramental presence of the living and exalted Lord in the Church.

It cannot be overlooked, moreover, that the Thomas incident
also relates to the problem of seeing and believing as they concern those who had never seen the historical Jesus and who consequently could not see as Thomas was privileged to see. In
apparent contrast to the experience of Thomas, Jesus speaks of
those as blessed "who have not seen and yet believe" (20:29).
This statement undoubtedly applies to the vast majority if not
the whole of those who are readers of the gospel, including the
readers of the present day. What of these? What of those to
whom the risen Lord does not appear and who had never known
Him in the flesh? John's answer is that they too must believe,
as Thomas believed, even though their experience in seeing differs
greatly from his own. They have not seen as Thomas saw. He
saw personally and physically. They must see through his witness and through that of the other apostles as that witness is recorded in the Scriptures. But in all cases, to that seeing must be
added the saving comprehension of what is seen. And that is
faith. In Christ's closing comments upon this incident, it is increasingly made evident that it is precisely the necessity for belief
in addition to sight and the possibility of such belief by means
of the Spirit which maintain the relevance of the gospel for the
generations of believers subsequent to that of the apostles.

With the contemporary problems in mind, John frequently
stresses the inadequacy of seeing apart from faith. Jesus' brothers
saw His works, yet they did not believe (7:3-5). Nor did the
vast majority of those who witnessed the multiplication of the
loaves (6:36). Most of the Jewish rulers did not believe although
they saw His miracles. And even at the resurrection of Lazarus
John contrasts the faith of those who believed in Christ with
the unbelief of those who reported the event, what they had only
seen physically, to the Pharisees (11:45, 46). In all of these
instances seeing and believing should belong together. There can
be no belief without some degree of sight, even if only through
the mediated testimony of eyewitnesses. Yet faith represents a
step beyond mere sight, and it is this step which constitutes the
difference between salvation and judgment for all who are concerned with Christ's claims through the witness of the apostles
and through the preaching and sacraments of the Church.

At this juncture, however, the theme of seeing and believing

resolves itself into another question which is really indicative of
the point at which this theme relates to the doctrine of the Spirit.
How does one go to faith from sight? What is the active ingre-
dient? And, practically speaking, why is it that some who see believe while others who also see reject the Gospel? That this is
a fundamental query for the evangelist is evident from the fact
that his account of Jesus' public ministry terminates on this theme,
pointing up the contrast between those who believed and the
larger number of those whose hearts were hardened (12:37-43).
John asks himself these questions and provides himself with answers, concluding that the unbelief of the nation was the result
of a divinely permitted hardening of their hearts in specific fulfillment of Isaiah's prophecy (Isaiah 6:10).

Moreover, the evangelist teaches as a complementary doctrine,
although not in chapter twelve, that belief is the consequence of
an equally supernatural, divine unveiling of God by Himself in
the heart of the one believing. Cullmann calls it "an act which
fulfills itself in the hearts of those who believe." [5] John's answer
to the problem of belief and unbelief is that there must be a
miracle. There must be new birth. And this reality, as Jesus
says to Nicodemus, is possible only through the impenetrable
working of God's Spirit (3:7, 8).

In the account of the healing of the blind man in chapter nine
John has provided an illustration of spiritual belief made possible
by a divine unveiling of the eyes. Nothing is more evident in
this story than the spiritual aspect of the miracle. For not only
does the blind man see; he comes to faith, his belief being contrasted at every point with the unbelief of the spiritual rulers of
the people. The rulers experience a spiritual hardening of their
hearts and in the end are pronounced blind by Jesus (9:40, 41).
The man who had been born blind goes on from faith to faith
and from sight to sight. At first the man born blind recognizes
Christ only as "the man called Jesus" (verse 11), then as a
prophet because he has performed a miracle (verse 17). Later,
in a second meeting with the rulers, the man confesses that Jesus
must be one who is sent from God (verse 33). Finally, when
Jesus reveals Himself to him for the first time after the healing,
the man comes to know Him as the Son of Man, the Christ, and
to worship Him as Lord (verses 35-38). The man born blind
then passes out of the picture as the typical believer, the forerunner of all believers, as one who has passed from Judaism to

Christianity and who now emerges as a witness to the One who effected the healing of his eyes. The point of the story is that his spiritual perception is preceded by a miracle, a miracle analogous to that performed in the hearts of all who believe by an equally supernatural (although spiritual) working of God's Spirit.

The Holy Spirit does not create the truth, nor is He Himself the object of God's revelation. Instead He creates the *vision* which is necessary if a blind man is to see the truth, and the life which is necessary if a dead man is to apprehend it. It is to be noted, however, that the reality which is anticipated by this miracle is really possible only in its fullness after the glorification of Jesus and the sending of the Spirit which attended upon that event. Since a true understanding of the events of Christ's life and ministry are possible only even for the disciples subsequent to the resurrection, it is impossible for the readers of the gospel to say that they are in an unfavorable position for understanding the meaning of Christ's life. On the contrary, as Cullmann points out, "They are to some extent in a preferable position to those who lived *only* in the time of the incarnate Christ," for the Spirit is now active to assist their understanding.[6]

A complementary doctrine to John's theme of seeing and believing lies in the gospel's insistence upon a divine predestination. The fact that this doctrine is so prominent is itself evidence of the interpretation given above of human faith. There is no belief without the prior working of God's Spirit. Christ's words can be heard only by those who have the God-given spiritual capacity for hearing. No one can come to Jesus unless the Father draws him (6:44). This is what the later Reformed theologians called unconditional election, and it is taught in the gospel in literally dozens of instances.

John says that those who believed in Christ "were born, not of blood nor of the will of the flesh nor of the will of man, but of God" (1:13), teaching that even the ability to believe is a divinely given faculty. In chapter three Jesus teaches that a spiritual rebirth (from above) is necessary if a man is to have eternal life. In chapter six Jesus says, "All that the Father gives me will come to me. . . . And this is the will of him who sent me, that I should lose nothing of all that he has given me" (6:37, 39). In chapter eight He declares that "he who is of God hears the words of God; the reason why you do not hear them is that you are not of God" (8:47). He tells the disciples, "You did not choose me, but I chose you. . . . If you were of the world, the world would love its own; but because you are not of the world, but I chose you out of the world, therefore the world hates you" (15:16, 19). In John 17 Christ speaks six times of those whom God has given Him (verses 2, 6, 11, 12 and 24) and distinguishes sharply between His own for whom He prays and the world, which is not His own and for whom He does not pray (verse 9). John teaches, therefore, that salvation depends upon Christ's Spirit. There is no salvation and there can be no salvation apart from this unexpected and unmerited activity of God.

THE PARACLETE

If the Spirit of Christ is really to be closely associated with the theme of seeing and believing, as John certainly seems to intimate, then the primary and normative function of the Paraclete must certainly be one of revelation. Christ's earthly life and atoning death were indeed the center of all saving revelation. But without the gradual illumination of the Spirit as far as men are concerned, this divine and perfect work remains entirely unintelligible and at least partly unobserved.

It has not always been recognized in the debate centering on the Paraclete how frequently the title the "Spirit of Truth" is used by John nor how closely associated the two terms are in the discourses which occupy chapters fourteen through sixteen of the gospel. If 16:7-11 and 16:12-15 are to be taken together, that is, as one extended logion on the Paraclete, then four separate Paraclete passages are to be distinguished—14:16-17; 14:25-26; 15:26-27 and 16:7-15. In each of these passages *paraklētos* is used once—in 14:16; 14:26; 15:26 and 16:7. In three of these instances the title "Spirit of Truth is also prominent. In the fourth the "Holy Spirit" occupies the parallel position.

Now the term "Spirit of Truth" is less enigmatic than Paraclete. It has already been observed in the present study in connection with the witness of Jesus Christ that "truth" in the Fourth Gospel denotes the essential nature of God or divine reality and that when John describes Jesus as the truth he means that Jesus Himself partakes of that divine reality and that His ministry really effects the revelation of that divine reality to men. The Scriptures contain this divine reality in words, and therefore they are true, just as Christ's signs are true and truth is characteristic of the prophetic and, therefore, God-inspired witness of the

Baptist (5:33). To speak of the Spirit as truth has, therefore, a twofold connotation. It means that the Spirit is the Spirit of God and of Jesus Christ, truth being the essential characteristic of His being. And it means that it is the Spirit who brings the truth and who gives true testimony, just as Jesus Himself speaks truth and gives true testimony. In this sense the Spirit's work is a work of revelation, designed to lead believers into spiritual reality, the opposite of every false appearance and belief.

Moreover, if these functions are actually carried out in the gospel, then the ministry of the Spirit must parallel the ministry of Christ Himself in most if not all of His functions. Such is actually the case. Christ has been sent to earth from heaven (3:17, 34; 5:24, 30, 36-38; 8:16 and many other texts). So also will the Spirit be sent from heaven (14:26; 15:26; 16:7). Christ came that He might make known the truth (7:16-18; 8:31, 32, 40-47). The Spirit will also reveal the truth to the disciples (16:13-15). Christ has an indirect ministry of judgment toward those who reject His message (9:39; 15:22-24). Similarly, the Spirit also exercises a ministry of judgment against the world in its unbelief (16:8-11). These examples indicate clearly that the Paraclete exercises a ministry that is parallel to that of Jesus Christ Himself.

At every point there is a slight difference, however. And this slight difference points to what is perhaps the most significant thing to be said about the Spirit. It is true that Christ is sent from heaven by the Father, but strictly speaking it is Christ who sends the Spirit (15:26; 16:7). Jesus testifies to the truth by bearing witness to Himself. The Spirit testifies to the truth by bearing witness to Jesus (15:26; 16:14). Finally, Jesus convicts the world of sin. But the Spirit convicts the world of sin through the witness of Christ's disciples to their Lord. These variations mean that the Spirit is *functionally* as well as *essentially* Christ's Spirit and, thus, is not and cannot be an independent authority in revelation. He testifies exclusively to Christ. His revelation is an extension of Christ's revelation. The Spirit is the revealer of Jesus. Jesus says that the Spirit "will not speak on his own authority, but whatever he hears he will speak. . . . He will glorify me, for he will take what is mine and declare it to you" (16:13, 14). "He will bear witness to me" (15:26). To these statements are to be added the references in the gospel to the fact that the disciples remembered the things which Jesus had done together with their spiritual significance after the resurrection (2:22; 12:16; 13:7).

The witness of the Spirit does not consist, then, in the perfecting of Christ's revelation by secret or mystical disclosures. He does not add to the revelation. The witness of the Spirit consists, first, in interpreting that revelation, given once in Christ, to the disciples and, second, in providing for the appropriation of it personally by those who believe through a hearing of the preaching of the Gospel. John is so certain that the features of Christ are to be seen in every manifestation of the Spirit in human testimony that in the first epistle he alludes to this factor as the criterion by which true prophets are to be distinguished from the spirit of antichrist (I John 4:2, 3).

In this second sense the Spirit is to provide for the appropriation of the revelation by all types of men in all periods of the Christian Church. The Spirit is the only possibility in virtue of which a man can speak of Christ. In this respect the witness of the Spirit is not the mystical communication of truth nor the emergence of a blind, purely subjective acceptance of a proposition. It is the gracious illumination of a mind darkened by sin so that the events of Christ's life and death are filled with their spiritual significance and the individual is enabled to embrace Jesus Christ to his salvation.

At this point it is naturally apparent in what sense John can use the word Paraclete as a title for the Spirit. The Spirit is the Spirit of revelation. He is Christ's witness, and hence, in a very real sense, His "advocate." The Spirit is never represented in the farewell discourses as the advocate of the disciples, pleading their cause with God or with the world. On the contrary, He is always the advocate of Christ, pleading Christ's cause with the disciples and in a different but closely related sense with unbelievers. To understand the word Paraclete in this sense allows one to adhere to the proper and only satisfactory meaning of the term, as many of the commentators on the gospel have clearly recognized.

Westcott writes that "in the Gospel again the sense of advocate, counsel, one who pleads, convinces, convicts, in a great controversy, who strengthens on the one hand and defends on the other, meeting formidable attacks, is alone adequate." [7] Dodd observes that *"paraklētos* is properly a forensic term. A paraclete is an advocate, who supports a defendant at his trial." [8] And

Bernard feels similarly that "the weight of evidence is undoubtedly in favor of 'advocate' rather than 'comforter' as the rendering of *paraklētos* in John." [9] It is an interesting point of evidence for this conclusion that the word was even borrowed directly from the Greek by the Jews and appears in the Talmudic writings in the sense of advocate. "He who does one precept gains for himself one advocate (*p^eraqlit*); and he who commits one transgression gains for himself one accuser" (Pirkē Aboth 4:13). Not all of these commentators recognize the Paraclete as the advocate of *Christ,* but it is in this sense that John primarily intends the term. As Christ's advocate the Spirit takes His place alongside of the other witnesses in John as bearing testimony exclusively to Jesus.

Moreover, this sense of the meaning of advocate is actually required by the content of chapters fourteen through fifteen of the gospel. In chapter fourteen the theme of consolation established in verse 1 ("Let not your hearts be troubled") and resumed in verse 18 ("I will not leave you desolate") has led many to the feeling that "Counselor" or "Comforter" is alone demanded as the translation of *paraklētos* in 14:16. But strictly speaking, the theme under discussion from verse 8 until the end of the chapter is the human possibility of knowing God, prefaced by Philip's request to see the Father—"Lord, show us the Father, and we shall be satisfied." Christ's answer is that the one who has seen Himself has seen the Father and that after His return to heaven the Spirit will perform the work of revelation. Thus, in verses 16 and 17 the coming of the Spirit to the disciples is introduced into the discourse, the mode of His operation being described ("You know him, for he dwells with you, and will be in you"), and in verse 26 it is explicitly stated that the revelation received through the Spirit will take the form of an illumination of the events of Christ's life and teaching. In other words, the statements of verses 16, 17, and 26 return to the thought contained in Philip's question, asserting that even after Jesus' death and His departure into heaven, the knowledge of God will still come through a knowledge of Jesus Himself and that this knowledge will be provided by the Spirit, who is Christ's advocate.

In chapters fifteen and sixteen the background of the discussion is more openly forensic with the result that the reference to the advocate is even more appropriate. In chapter fifteen it must be remembered that the Paraclete passage is immediately preceded by a pointed summation of the world's unbelief, against which Christ's words (verse 22), his works (verse 24), the Paraclete (verse 26), and the disciples themselves (verse 27) appear as witnesses. All of these witnesses are witnesses to Christ, and all have at least a semi-judicial bearing in their reference to the world. Similarly, in chapter sixteen the Paraclete is introduced as Christ's advocate against the world, convincing it "of sin and of righteousness and of judgment" (verse 8), thereby fulfilling a function which is parallel to that of Christ Himself (9: 39; 15:22-24). In the final discourses the Spirit is truly Christ's advocate, just as Christ is the advocate of the Father (14:16).

It is certainly to be asked at this point, however, why it is that the evangelist has chosen a word like Paraclete to describe this function of the Spirit. It is not without meaning when considered in the context of the discourses, but one cannot help feeling that a word like "teacher," "witness" or "revealer" would have been more appropriate and would have given less cause for misunderstanding and misinterpretation. This question is important, and the answers to it really contain the final solution to the problem of the Paraclete in John.

In the first place, it must be noticed that John exhibits a rather consistent interest in legal terms among which *paraklētos* is neither inappropriate nor unexpected: accuse, convict, testify, defend, and judge. Since the Spirit is one of the witnesses to Christ presented in the gospel, it is not at all strange that John should have settled upon *paraklētos* as a congenial designation of His function.

It is also to be noted that a strictly forensic function of the Spirit is not lacking in many other New Testament and apocryphal passages and that John's selection of a legal title is, therefore, not so much of an innovation as it appears. The term may be new (although it may be considerably older than is known to scholars), but the forensic setting of the Spirit's work is not new. Thus, in Mark 13:9-13 and parallels, Jesus warns the disciples of persecution, adding that in the hour of judgment the Holy Spirit will teach them what they shall say. In Romans 8 Paul speaks of the persuasive power of the Spirit who Himself bears "witness with our spirit that we are children of God" (verse 16). This Spirit "intercedes for us with sighs too deep for words" (verse 26). It is not without interest that John also speaks of a threefold witness to Jesus in the first epistle, that of "the Spirit, the water, and the blood" (I. John 5:8), and that the Testament of Judah recognizes two spirits—the spirit of truth and the spirit of deceit—noting that "the spirit of truth testifieth all things, and accuseth all; and the sinner is burnt up by his own heart, and cannot raise his face to the judge" (20:5).

In the third place, it is quite to the point that the word Paraclete has other associations than merely advocate, for while the revelational function of the Spirit is central in the final discourses it is not correct to hold that this function is the only one that is found there. If the word may mean comforter as well as advocate, this variation is singularly appropriate, especially in the last discourses where the sorrow of the disciples at the thought of Jesus' departure is a poignant and recurring theme. The same is true of the thought of "helper," and above all of "teacher" or "exhorter," the theme which Barrett expounds in his approach to the Paraclete sayings.[10] According to Barrett, *parakletos* may be understood in connection with *parakalein* ("exhort") and *paraklesis* ("exhortation"), both of which refer to prophetic Christian preaching and may, therefore, designate the Spirit as one who exhorts the disciples by declaring to them the things of Christ. This meaning comes closer than any other to expressing precisely the function of the Spirit as interpreter of the teachings and the ministry of Jesus. The fact that the word may have these auxiliary meanings does not imply that the translation "advocate" should be rejected; but it does provide a warning against interpreting the Spirit's functions in too rigid or too limited a manner. As Hoskyns with his admirable theological sensitivity perceives, "What is perhaps more important than the actual choice of this translation or of that, is that the word chosen should not be such as to appear to limit the active functions of the Spirit of Truth, whether towards the disciples or towards the world, or to obscure the fact that these functions are complementary and issue directly from the nature of God's act of Revelation in Christ, whose Word is a two-edged sword." [11]

The final answer to why John describes the Spirit as the Paraclete lies in the function which the Spirit manifests to the world. John calls it one of "conviction" and develops the theme most fully in 16:8-11. There he writes, "And when he comes, he will convince the world of sin and of righteousness and of judgment: of sin, because they do not believe in me; of righteousness, because I go to the Father, and you will see me no more; of judgment, because the ruler of this world is judged." This function is so clearly a forensic activity that the title Paraclete may clearly be said to belong primarily to it just as the title Spirit of Truth belongs primarily to the Spirit's activity in revelation.

To convict someone of something is a classical construction, the verb signifying "to confute, refute," "to bring to light by cross examination." The work of the Spirit is, therefore, to expose, or bring to light the true state of the world's wickedness in relation to its sin and Christ's righteousness. The sin, as John notes, consists in the rejection of Jesus (3:18-21; 9:41; 11:37-40). The conviction of the Spirit in relation to the world's sin consists in making the things of Christ so evident that the rejection of them or unbelief is clearly revealed for what it is. Similarly, the righteousness is the righteousness of Christ, the meaning captured by the Sinaic Syriac which reads, "He will reprove the world in its sins and about *His* righteousness" at verse 8. This means that the standard of God's righteousness will be established against the unrighteousness of the world by the Spirit in His work of illuminating the person and the teachings of the Lord. It is in association with the two previous illuminations that the world is also convicted of judgment, both of the justice of God's judgments and of their present realization. Here Christ looks forward to His passion seeing in it that exposure of right and wrong which is to go on throughout the course of history as the result of the ever fuller extension of the preaching of the Gospel.

In the final analysis, therefore, the conviction of the world of sin, righteousness, and judgment takes place through the witness of the Church, through its preaching and its sacraments, as through these the Spirit bears His intangible witness to the Lord. In this supernatural work the believers and, in the first instance, the apostles become God's instrument. The Spirit operates in them. The witness of the Spirit works itself out in the witness of the apostles. In this sense the Paraclete becomes in some measure the advocate of the disciples, but He is so only because He is first the advocate of Christ and because both He and the believers are united in the same work of proclamation. It is evident also from the previous descriptions that the two-sided function of the Spirit—to illuminate the meaning of Christ's death and ministry for the disciples and for all believers and to convict the world of its sins and of Christ's righteousness unto judgment

—is not in reality a double function, but a single ministry, justifying the evangelist's use of the titles Paraclete and Spirit of Truth for both sides of this activity.

Hoskyns writes that "God sent His Son into the world through love for the world, but the rejection of God's love in the Jesus of history brings man under judgment. Consequently the Spirit of Truth, just because He reveals God's love and assures men of it, Himself exposes the blindness and darkness of the world." [12] This twofold consequence takes place, according to the fourth evangelist, whenever and wherever the Spirit testifies, wherever Christ is set forth to the gaze of men and whenever believers bear their witness to the eternally relevant and saving power of the Christian revelation.

Appendix

The Johannine conception of the incarnate Logos has been extensively investigated in many recent studies and has for the most part been adequately treated in the major commentaries. The parallels to the idea in contemporary and pre-Christian literature are multiple. It is, however, as much an error to regard these parallels or any one of them exclusively as the source of the Johannine Logos concept as it is to regard the concept itself as one which dominates the gospel.

Many of the ideas in the prologue are understandable upon Old Testament presuppositions and upon the Old Testament significance of the "word (*dabar*) of God." In addition to purely formal usage, the divinely spoken "word" is used in the Old Testament of the creative and sustaining power of God (Gen. 1:3 ff.; Psalms 33:6; 107:20). Repo speaks of the "dynamic" coloring of *dabar*, stressing its translation in some cases as "deed."[1] In the instances just cited God's word is His act. In many cases *dabar* is best rendered by the English words for "thing," "event," or "happening," as "the thing comes from the Lord" (Gen. 24: 50). In its creative faculty God's word possesses the power of self-realization (Isa. 55:10, 11).

A second group of passages uses *dabar* of God's divine revelation to Israel given through the priests and prophets (Isa. 9:8; Jer. 1:4; 20:8; Ezek. 1:3; Amos 3:1, 8), in which the term is to be identified in some measure with the Torah (for which see Isa. 2:3 where "law" and "word" occur together in parallel construction). With these points the Johannine doctrine of the Logos is quite familiar, and many scholars have noted the deliberate attempt by John to link the Logos with the creative word of

Genesis 1. That John writes in this context is not insignificant. His conception makes use of the Old Testament ideas of the self-revealing word. But the orthodox Old Testament figure did not conceive of God's word as a distinctive entity existing alongside of God from the beginning nor of the sublime movement of such an hypostasis from a position as mediator of creation to the assumption of flesh in the act of revelation and reconciliation. The approaches to a personification of the word in Psalms 33:6; 107: 20; 147:15 and Isaiah 55:10 f. are no exception, the language being clearly poetic, not realistic or even mythological.

The idea of a mediating divine hypostasis may be paralleled more closely in various aspects of Judaistic thought and of the intertestamental literature which preceded it, but there is nothing here to equal the force or originality of the Johannine conception. Thus, the Wisdom of Solomon refers to the Word as a bellicose mediator of the divine will—

> Thine all-powerful word leaped from heaven down from
>   the royal throne,
> A stern warrior, into the midst of the doomed land

(Wisdom 18:15; cf. also Wisdom 9:1 and 16:12)—and speaks even more objectively of Wisdom as a semi-divine figure whose source is in God and whose activities include the creation of the world, its preservation, and the inspiration and purification of men (Wisdom 7:22–8:3; 9:4, 9-11). In the time of the evangelist this later conception was apparently widespread, as many references in the Old Testament and in the apocryphal literature would indicate: Job 28:12-28; Proverbs 8:1–9:18; IV Ezra 5:10; I Baruch 3:9–4:4; Sirach 1:1-10, 14-20; 24:1-22; 51:13-30; I Enoch 42; II Enoch 30:8. Yet in spite of its currency, it remains questionable whether Wisdom is an adequate source to explain the Johannine shift from personification to personalization. It is generally true that these passages are more poetic than personalistic, and any serious personalization would be radically alien to the prevailing Jewish perspective which saw Wisdom as inseparable from the Torah (I Baruch 4:1, 2; cf. Sirach 19:20-22). According to Kittel, who provides an extensive list of parallels between the prologue and rabbinical statements about the Torah, John is even conscious of this contrast when he emphasizes that Christ is the new Torah who by His personal incarnation supersedes the Torah which has preceded Him. It may also be noted that on the assumption that Wisdom is the source of the Johannine concept it is even difficult to explain why John should have substituted the Logos title for Wisdom itself, the original and more easily identifiable figure.

Both the related "Truth myth" of Judaism, which Bultmann cites in his commentary as a late parallel to the prologue, and the *memra Yahweh* of the Targums, which Hamp, Strack-Billerbeck, and others have carefully investigated, also fail to account for the Johannine personalization. The latter, as Strack-Billerbeck observes in a prolonged excursus and as Moore agrees, never translates such phrases as "the word (*dabar*) of the Lord" or "the word of God."[2] In fact, as Hamp maintains, *memra* in the Targums, although a common and stylistic expression, exhibits no fixed system, and the *memra* of Yahweh and the Johannine Logos, while both rooted in the Old Testament themes and traditions, have no direct bearing upon each other. *Memra* does not refer to a divine mediator of God or of the divine revelation. In the light of Hamp's extensive investigation, Barrett is justified in terming *memra* "a blind alley in the study of the biblical background of John's Logos doctrine."[3]

The incarnation is also the sticking place in regard to Philo's Logos. That Philo had a conception of an hypostasized "Word of God" based upon Platonic and later Stoic philosophy, the principal concept being the "reason" both above (Plato) and in (Stoics) the world, to which, especially in its cosmological aspects, some of the Johannine statements are similar is not to be denied. But there are striking differences between John and Philo, and few would maintain that John shares Philo's speculative interest or that Philo ever speaks explicitly of the Logos as a person in the Johannine sense. The pure logos of Philo is the logos of the Greek philosophers and belongs to the incorruptible world of higher reality. It could never have endured an incarnation into corruptible matter.

John's Logos becomes the incarnate revealer of light and life to men. It is significant in this respect that Origen, whose thought developed within the Alexandrine school and whose knowledge of Philo was certainly a sympathetic one, saw the dominant ideas of the prologue (including the Logos) to lie, not in Philo or in Greek philosophy, but in the sphere of Jewish thought and interest.[4] The significance of the study of Philo's doctrine lies in the illumination of the type of popular speculation with which John, in presenting his new conception, assumes his readers to have been familiar. "The relevant evidence seems to show that in circles with which the evangelist and his readers may be supposed to have been in touch the conception of a mediating divine hypostasis or hypostases was extremely widespread, and that in some such circles the term *logos* was used to denote such an hypostasis."[5]

In a number of recent studies, the source of the Johannine Logos has been found in the mythology of Hellenistic gnosticism or in the conceptions of neo-Pythagorean and neo-Platonic philosophy. Here the revelational and soteriological aspects of the prologue are easily paralleled. But the basic conception of a good world marred by sin so characteristic of the biblical cosmology is lacking in nearly all forms of Gnostic speculation, and it is significant that the Fourth Gospel presents the Word as object acting in history rather than the subject of esoteric knowledge or religious contemplation.

In the light of the preceding discussion it can be said that the Johannine doctrine of the Logos should surprise the reader not for its occurrence nor for the grandeur of its statements concerning Jesus Christ—there are ample related ideas in many of the thought systems of the times—but for the fact that it has attained such distinctive form despite the obvious pressures only to echo a prevailing mode of thought. The answer to this puzzle lies in the fact of the incarnation itself and in the hold that this reality maintained on the mind of the evangelist. Thus, Bultmann especially, but also others, proceed wrongly when they ask for the source of the Johannine concept and search for an answer in contemporary texts. Christ Himself is the source. The idea is there. It includes the pre-existence of Christ, His divinity, His activity in creation, His person as the source of life and light, the incarnation, and the soteriological and revelational aspects of His ministry on earth.

All of these aspects of the meaning of Jesus are affirmed or at least implied in Christ's own teaching as recorded in the gospel. To communicate these ideas John avails himself of a term well known to his contemporaries through Palestinian, Alexandrian, and Hellenistic schemes of thought. Consequently, these systems are to be investigated, not as sources of the Johannine conception, but for the implications and overtones which they provide to the prologue and which were played upon by the evangelist in this unique expression of the significance of Jesus Christ. Hamp observes that "the Johannine prologue with its Logos reveals something new in terms of content; by it a hellenistic term is Christianized, and the Word of creation is clearly made known. The doctrine of truth of the Old Testament is worked into the speculation."[6]

Considered from this perspective the Logos parallels are striking. To the Greeks especially, but also to the Jews, the description of Christ as Logos points emphatically to His pre-existent state as Son of God and mediator of the creation. In John's thought, however, the conception rises far above that of a mere son of God, a figure who partakes in some measure of God's nature, to describe the Son *par excellence*—eternally existing with God, partaking in its fullness of the divine nature, and acting with God in the creation (verse 3) and the preservation of the world (verse 4). To the Jew the "word" recalls creative action, action which is at once a revelation of God's person and of His inscrutable will. John adds, however, that the revelation in Christ, God's perfect Word, reveals as no other the fullness of God's glory in its aspects of grace and truth (verse 14) and is that which above all else summons men to repentance and to the acceptance of light and life through Him.

The Logos terminology rises to new heights in John in expressing a twofold significance of Jesus Christ—the significance of His person in its pre-existent and incarnate states and the significance of His ministry as an act of revelation and reconciliation. All this John does without in the least distracting from the importance of the historical Jesus as the focal point of the divine disclosure. For whatever may have been the teachings about the Logos in the first Christian century, it is John's first and distinctive teaching that *Jesus,* not another, is the divine hypostasis who had been with God from all eternity, who was God, and who took on human form by incarnation, appearing on earth for the saving revelation of the Father, and that the Logos, in spite of contemporary teaching and the philosophical speculations attaching to it, is only to be found in this historical personage and at this moment in history in which He made His person known.

Notes

CHAPTER 1

[1] G. C. Berkouwer, *General Revelation* (Eerdmans, 1964), p. 89.

[2] *Ibid.*, p. 98.

[3] Wolfhart Pannenberg, *Offenbarung als Geschichte* (Vandenhoeck & Ruprecht, 1963), p. 92.

[4] The debate about the witness terminology originates in a pioneering article by Kattenbusch for the *Zeitschrift fuer die neutestamentliche Wissenschaft* (4 [1903], pp. 111-127), drawing attention to the fact that scholars had not yet explained how the martyrs of the early Church came to receive the title of *martys* ("witness"), a word that originally had nothing to do with the suffering of death for one's beliefs. The author proposed two possible solutions — first, that the martyr was called by this title because he was believed to be the possessor of special knowledge communicated by the Holy Spirit and possibly mediated in a vision in the hour of his death to which he alone was able to bear witness and, second, that a true witness was conceived to be an imitator of Jesus Christ, especially unto death. Kattenbusch was unsatisfied with these explanations himself. Seven years later Geffcken applied a form of literary analysis coupled with a history-of-religions approach to the martyr accounts and arrived at a third and completely new solution (*Hermes*, 45 [1910], pp. 481-505). Geffcken found the martyr acts, including the accounts of Christ's trial before Pilate, to follow the literary pattern of the Greek philosopher trials (Socrates, Thrasea Paetus, Helvidius Priscus, Rubellius Plautus, and Seneca) where the persistence in a position or a belief meant certain death. Hence, the martyr title came directly from this process. Holl and Lietzmann later amplified upon Geffcken's work by distinguishing two forms of martyr documents — the letter and the trial — instead of one.

In 1914 and the years immediately following, the discussion of the martyr title erupted in a multiplicity of articles by Holl, Corsen and Reitzenstein, the last two writing in opposition to a new thesis proposed by Holl (*Gesammelte Aufsaetze zur Kirchengeschichte II, Der Osten*, 1928, pp. 68-114). Holl approached the problem as a historian, affirming that

165

martys was originally a title of honor for an apostle — as a prophet who had seen the risen Lord. He supported this view by arguing for the existence of the title *martys tou Theou* from I Corinthians 15:15, where the negative ascription (*pseudomartyres tou Theou*) occurs. When it came to be believed about the beginning of the second century that martyrs, such as Stephen, saw the risen Lord and were able to foretell the future, the martyr title passed inevitably to them. In proposing this thesis the author was a bit highhanded with Kattenbusch whose approach, he maintained, had made the martyr problem unjustifiably difficult. Since that time most scholars have found Holl to have made it unjustifiably simple and have rejected his conclusions.

Corsen, who opposed Holl, linked the confession of the martyr before the pagan tribunal with the baptismal ritual of the Christian congregations and conceived of the believer as taking the place of his master, as a slave under ancient law could do for his lord (*Neue Jahrbuecher fuer das klassische Altertum*, 35 [1915], pp. 481-501). The title thus refers, not to secret knowledge, but to simple confession. Reitzenstein also insisted on witness as a vocalized confession along the pattern established by the Hellenistic philosophers (such as Epictetus). He found the true martyr to be an imitator of Jesus Christ (*Nachrichten von der koeniglichen Gesellschaft der Wissenschaften zu Goettingen*, philologisch-historische Klasse, 1916, pp. 417-467).

In the midst of this exchange Schlatter, in 1915, proposed an explanation of the martyr problem on the basis of Judaistic documents, in which the sufferings and the deaths of the prophets are quite prominent (*Der Maertyrer in den Anfangen der Kirche*, 1915). Since the prophets were known as witnesses for God and since their fate was usually one of martyrdom (a belief reflected in Matt. 5:12; 23:30; Acts 7:51, 52; Heb. 11: 35-38 and James 5:10), the title of witness in the sense of martyr passed in a natural way to the apostles and to their followers in the Church. This explanation was in general agreement with that of Holl but without Holl's unfortunate emphasis upon the title. Shortly after this Krueger explained the title as an instance of a "deed-witness" on the basis of I Clement 5, I Timothy 6:11ff. and Eusebius II, xxiii, 18; III, xxxii, 6; IV, xxii, 4, thereby becoming the first to apply philological criteria to the martyr problem (*Zeitschrift fuer die neutestamentliche Wissenschaft*, 17 [1916], pp. 264-269). With Krueger the first stage of the debate drew to an end with all of the major lines of approach made evident.

In the second stage of the debate the previous possibilities were generally revived and defended with new arguments by a wide variety of scholars—Delehaye, Dornseiff, Lohmeyer, Michel, Guenther, Manson, Casey and others.

The final stage in the development of the discussion is seen in the appearance of more comprehensive works in which the previous contributions are correlated and the boundaries of the debate enlarged. Such are Campenhausen's study of *Die Idee des Martyriums in der alten Kirche* (Vandenhoeck & Ruprecht, 1964), the extended article on *"Martys"* by Strathmann for the Kittel *Theological Dictionary of the New Testament*, and the latest and most complete of the studies on *Zeuge und Maertyrer*

(Kösel-Verlag, 1961) by Brox. With Campenhausen the first clear distinction occurs between a witness to the facts and a witness to a person, a distinction as basic to the witness concepts as that between a witness by words and a witness by deeds which Campenhausen also observes. Strathmann phrases the same distinction as a witness to the facts versus a witness to opinions, using the distinction extensively in his careful investigation of the New Testament texts. Brox's contribution consists in a perceptive and extensive review of the previous studies and in the welcome association of the witness terms with a number of closely related subjects, such as the themes of authority and unbelief in John.

[5] George Foot Moore, *Judaism in the First Centuries of the Christian Era: The Age of the Tannaim*, III (Harvard, 1962), p. 83.

[6] To the present writer it seems a questionable procedure to amplify the significance of such a religious witness by reference to the modern distinction between religious and non-religious truth, as Strathmann appears to do in his discussion of the texts for the Kittel *Theological Dictionary of the New Testament*. Strathmann acknowledges that for the prophets the divinity of God and his special salvation acts in history are facts, yet not facts which can be observed and legally established. They are facts which are only certain to the eyes of faith (*ibid.*, IV, p. 484). Whatever the validity of this modern differentiation may be, it seems singularly inappropriate to the text at hand. Those who are called upon to witness are, not only those of Israel, but the people of all nations, and all are asked to defend their worship of other gods by the right of these gods to receive worship on the basis of their revelational and soteriological activity (43:12). This is an argument from history (cp. also the similar passage in 41:21-29), and the thought undoubtedly rests upon Israel's possession of the law and her preservation as a nation throughout the centuries. Certainly religious truth is involved, especially in the ultimate fact to be established, but the argument is not divorced from verifiable experience. It would be more correct to say that in these verses, as throughout the Old Testament generally, religious and non-religious truth are indissolubly united and that the ultimate religious truth — the identity of the one true God — is established upon an experience in history which is not totally unlike the historical experience of the heathen nations.

[7] As a Greek translation of *'eduth, mo'ed*, and to a lesser extent also of *'ed* and *'edah* in the Septuagint, *martyrion* assumes an importance in the Greek Old Testament which is unparalleled by any one of the original words in the Hebrew text. The word occurs about 250 times in all, about 100 times in translations of the phrase *'ohel mo'ed* ("the tabernacle of meeting") and many other times to render "his testimonies," "the tabernacle of the testimony," "the ark of the testimony" and related phrases. In the majority of instances it relates primarily to the self-revelation of God. As a translation of *mo'ed, martyrion* is, of course, a technical error, although not an inappropriate one. To the reader of the Septuagint, *martyrion* would thus combine under one term ideas that were not nearly so united in the actual Hebrew text of the Old Testament, and as a result the version may be presumed to have had an influence on the development of the theology of the law in inter-testamental and later Judaism to

the extent that the later development was influenced by the Greek version of the Scriptures. It is not impossible that the translation was itself influenced by the beginning of the development of a rabbinic doctrine of the law in the period between the return of the Jews to Palestine and the translation of Scripture for the use of the Diaspora. It is to be observed that in spite of the prominence of the word in the Septuagint and the familiarity which John may be presumed to have had with the Greek translation, the development of the idea of witness in the Fourth Gospel does not depend on it lexically at least, since, with the sole exception of Revelation 15:5 where the word occurs in the stereotyped phrase "the tabernacle of the testimony," *martyrion* does not occur in the entire Johannine corpus.

CHAPTER 2

[1] Marcus Barth, *Der Augenzeuge* (Evangelischer Verlag, 1946), p. 272.

[2] Karl Barth, *Der Christ als Zeuge* (Kaiser Verlag, 1934), pp. 7, 8.

[3] In Matthew and Mark the word group adheres closely to the forensic meaning of the terms. In Matthew 18:16 *martys* is used of the "two or three witnesses" which were necessary for the establishment of fact in Jewish jurisprudence (Num. 35:30; Deut. 17:6; 19:15) — a similar reference is intended in Acts 7:58 — and at Christ's trial the words "witness" and "false witness" are used of Christ's accusers. Similarly, *martyria* denotes the adverse testimony produced against Jesus at his trial. Christ's command that the former leper present himself with an offering before the high priests — "for a *testimony* unto them" (Mark 1:44) — exhibits the same forensic basis. A special use of *martyrion* pictures a symbolic act as a prosecution witness against a person or group of persons in view of the final judgment (Mark 6:11; 13:9; Matt. 24:14; James 5:3 and parallels).

The Synoptic writers speak generally of forensic witness, especially of witness before an authorized tribunal. *Martys* denotes one who testifies in a judicial setting; *martyrein*, the act of giving testimony; *martyria*, the witnessing itself; and *martyrion*, the evidence objectively considered, especially as that which will appear at the last assize.

In the Pauline corpus the student of the New Testament encounters a much greater variety of terms and an increased range of applications. Although not so closely restricted to testimony in court, Paul's use of the word group to describe human testimony to a fact falls within the scope of the forensic viewpoint characteristic of the Synoptics (Rom. 10:2; II Cor. 8:3; Gal. 4:15). Paul can also use the same words to mean "proclaim" or "make known" (I Cor. 15:15; Gal. 5:3; I Thess. 4:6; I Tim. 2:6) or of human character, whether attested by men (I Tim. 3:7; 5:10; 6:12, 13) or by the human conscience (Rom. 2:15; 9:1; II Cor. 1:12). Parallel with the first variation is the apostle's use of *martyrion* to designate the gospel. Thus, Paul writes of the "testimony of Christ" (I Cor. 1:6), the "testimony of God" (I Cor. 2:1), "our testimony" (II Thess. 1:10), and the "testimony of our Lord" (II Tim. 1:8; for which compare Rom.

1:16). It is hard to deny that in these cases the word group has begun to acquire religious, and even revelational overtones.

4 Hermann Strathmann, "*Martys, k. t. l.,*" *Theological Dictionary of the New Testament,* ed. by Gerhard Kittel, IV (Eerdmans, 1967), p. 493 and Lucien Cerfaux, "Témoins du Christ," *Angelicum,* 20 (1943), pp. 166-183.

5 Hans Freiherr von Campenhausen, *Die Idee des Martyriums in der alten Kirche* (Vandenhoeck & Ruprecht, 1964), p. 31.

6 The vision is significant to Corssen who considers both Stephen and Philip, who also received a vision, to be personalities "bordering on the Apostolate" ("Begriff und Wesen des Maertyrers in der alten Kirche," *Neue Jahrbuecher fuer das klassische Altertum,* 35 [1915], p. 31). Strathmann, however, feels inclined to consider Stephen a martyr, although not in the later sense of that word ("Stephen is not called a witness because he dies; he dies because he is a witness of Christ and because of his evangelistic activity," *op. cit.,* p. 494). Brox finds a solution in a departure from the normal Lukan usage to the earlier "word witness" of Paul (*Zeuge und Maertyrer,* Kösel-Verlag, 1961, pp. 59, 60). To the present writer Brox's frank admission of a departure from the normal Lukan usage is most attractive, especially when it is remembered that the idea of a "word witness" is included rather than excluded in the conception of apostolic testimony. There is no reason, moreover, why the passage, since it occurs in a speech of Paul, may not embody Pauline rather than Lukan terminology.

7 An excellent discussion of the Johannine vocabulary for revelation involving many of these terms can be found in Hugo H. Huber, *Der Begriff der Offenbarung im Johannes-Evangelium* (Vandenhoeck & Ruprecht, 1934), p. 72 ff.

8 Bo Reicke, *Neutestamentliche Zeitgeschichte* (Alfred Töpelmann, 1965), p. 227.

CHAPTER 3

1 In the course of his studies of the Fourth Gospel Bultmann has been greatly impressed with the Johannine interpretation of Christ's ministry and has attempted to explain it by a characteristic appeal to Gnostic speculation. "The figure of Jesus in John is portrayed in the forms offered by the Gnostic Redeemer-myth. . . . Jesus appears as in the Gnostic myth as the pre-existent Son of God whom the Father clothed with authority and sent into the world" (*Theology of the New Testament,* II [Scribners, 1955], pp. 12, 13). That this is the general Johannine teaching may hardly be doubted, but it is unnecessary to appeal to Gnostic mythology in explanation of the Johannine frame of thought. The idea would be latent in any system which maintains a belief in revealed religion, and there are frequent examples of such a belief in divine messengers in antiquity. In Acts 14:8-18, for instance, the Greek inhabitants of Lystra in Lycaonia were so impressed by the healing of a cripple by the apostle Paul that they identified Barnabas with Zeus and Paul, who was the chief speaker, with Mercury, the divine messenger of the gods. Moreover, even in

Judaism there is a sense in which the prophet stands as a messenger between two worlds and proclaims to this world what he has observed in
the council chambers of heaven. The fact that the two witnesses of Revelation appear in exactly this capacity (Rev. 11:3-13) indicates that the
conception was not far removed from the thought patterns of the New
Testament writers.

2 Hugo H. Huber, *Der Bergriff der Offenbarung im Johannes-Evangelium*
(Vandenhoeck & Ruprecht, 1934), pp. 101-123.

3 *Ibid.*, p. 102.

4 Bernard Weiss, *Biblical Theology of the New Testament*, II (T. & T.
Clark, 1885), p. 332.

5 Ignace de la Potterie, *"Oida* et *ginōskō:* Les deux modes de la con-
naissance dans le quatrième Évangile," *Biblica,* 40 (1959), pp. 715, 716.

6 The use of four plural verb forms in this verse has been a source of
difficulty for commentators and has occasioned various explanations. The
most ambitious has been that of Lyder Brun. In two articles for *Symbolae
Osloenses* Brun maintains that the superior knowledge of Jesus and the
witness resulting from it depend in no way upon Christ's pre-incarnate
existence with the Father and His memory of it but upon what He knows
of the Father in and by His present communion with Him in His incarnate
state. Thus, the "we" of 3:11 refers to all who know the truth as Christ
did — through the Spirit. This view is supported by the contention that
an earthly perception is intended in every instance in which John speaks
of a "hearing" or "seeing" by Jesus (i.e., of hearing in 5:19f., 31f., 37;
8:40; 14:10, 24; 15:15; 16:13; 17:8, 14 and of seeing in 1:18; 5:19; 6:46
and 8:38) and by the interpretation of "heavenly things" in 3:11, 12 to
indicate, not the new birth itself and the teachings associated with it, but
the necessity of the new birth which all who believe apparently would
come or would have come to recognize. Brun's interpretation means that
Jesus' knowledge of heavenly things differed in degree but not in kind or
substance from the spiritual perception of all believers and that His messianic consciousness, whatever it may have been, was based not upon an
awareness of a previous existence with the Father but upon a consciousness of divine Sonship acquired in this life. Such a view falls short of the
Johannine presentation.

In the first place, even granting Brun's contentions about the passage
in chapter three, it is almost undeniable that John often intends to teach
that Christ's existence with God in heaven before the incarnation was
the foundation for His earthly activity as the revealer. This idea is certainly present in the prologue, and it is applied in so many additional
texts relating to the hearing or seeing of Jesus that Brun's attempt to re-
interpret the literal meaning of these passages is overshadowed by the
bulk of their number alone. Secondly, even if Christ's knowledge of certain "heavenly things" is to be taken as a knowledge gained on earth, this
conclusion still does not argue against the fact that Christ's superior knowledge of these things may only have been possible because His pre-incarnate
existence endowed Him with qualities not possessed by fallen men and that
His continual growth in this knowledge was assured by His unwavering con-

viction of a heavenly origin and a divine commission. Godet, for instance, maintains in his commentary both a certain growth in earthly knowledge by Jesus and His certainty of a messianic calling. Finally, if the majority of the passages in the gospel which deal with Jesus' knowledge are to be taken as teaching a knowledge based on His heavenly existence, it becomes exceedingly improbable that Brun's interpretation can even be accepted for the statements in 3:11-13, where consistency would itself require an interpretation more in accordance with the rest of the Johannine utterances.

In actual fact, the "we" is not as hard to explain as Brun's extensive treatment would indicate. In varying degrees Westcott, Bernard, and Dodd, relate the corporate witness to the witness of the Church, not in the sense of adding to Christ's witness, as if the Church possessed a revelation or a claim to revelation of her own, but as an increasingly perceptive and unfolding proclamation of Christ's own revelation as the meaning of that revelation is declared to the Church by the persisting ministry of the Holy Spirit (14:26; 16:13-15). The plural forms can, therefore, refer, as they must, to the knowledge of those who have believed in Jesus, to the disciples and to those who follow them in faith. These know on the basis of Christ's original and unique knowledge and not on any intuitive knowledge of their own. The speaking and the witnessing of verse eleven are in the present tense to indicate that the revelation brought and declared by Christ is constantly proclaimed in the Christian community on the basis of Christ's own knowledge of the Father.

⁷ In a stimulating discussion of these texts in *Zeuge und Maertyrer* (Kösel-Verlag, 1961, pp. 73-75) Brox maintains that in both cases the witness of Jesus moves on another plane and with other assumptions than that of human testimony, and that in neither case does Jesus meet the requirements of the argument demanded by His opponents. In chapter five "the other" of verse 32 is rightly taken to be the Father whose double witness consists in the evidence of the works and Scripture, but neither of these citations, according to Brox, supports the case as it must be argued before men. Similarly, the double witness of the Father and the Son in chapter eight (verse 18) bears only a formal approximation to the popular understanding of a witness and his testimony.

In reply to Brox's contention it should be clearly acknowledged that the testimony presented by Christ certainly moves to a higher level than would be expected in a case of Jewish law. Christ deals with revelation and with the validation of religious claims. But the acknowledgment of this fact should not be permitted to obscure the human nature of the argument. In chapter five Jesus produces supplementary witnesses among which, together with the works and Scripture, is John the Baptist. In the case of John especially, but also in that of the works and Scripture, the evidence falls within the sphere of human verification as the Jews themselves recognized when they sent representatives to John to hear his message (verse 33). In chapter eight, by contrast, the argument is obviously a spiritual one, but even as such it presupposes the rabbinic principles. Here the variation is to be found in the subject of the debate and not in a departure from the popular usage of the terms. As Hoskyns notes, "If in a

criminal investigation a matter be established at the mouth of two human witnesses . . . it follows *a fortiori* that, in an investigation concerning the action of God for the salvation of his people, the matter is finally
established by the combined witness of the Father and the Son" (*The
Fourth Gospel*, Faber and Faber, 1961, p. 332). Christ's thought is not
one-sided. He submits to the requirements of human witness but at the
same time carries the principles so involved into the realm of spiritual
verities in which men are called upon to acknowledge without qualification the faithful and unbroken word of God.

[8] Bultmann, *op. cit.*, I, pp. 26-32.

[9] Oscar Cullmann, *Salvation in History* (Harper & Row, 1967), pp. 197, 198.

[10] Ernst Kaesemann, *Essays on New Testament Themes*, "Studies in
Biblical Theology," 41 (S. C. M., 1964), p. 43. Cf. also pp. 37-45.

[11] Guenther Bornkamm, *Jesus of Nazareth* (Hodder & Stoughton, 1963), pp. 172-178.

[12] Oscar Cullmann, *The Christology of the New Testament* (S. C. M., 1963), p. 8.

[13] Weiss, *op. cit.*, II, p. 352.

[14] Bultmann, *op. cit.*, II, p. 62.

[15] *Ibid.*, II, p. 63.

[16] C. H. Dodd, *The Interpretation of the Fourth Gospel* (Cambridge, 1963), p. 384.

[17] Emil Brunner, *Revelation and Reason* (Westminster, 1946), p. 110.

[18] Karl Barth, *Church Dogmatics*, I, 1 (T. & T. Clark, 1960), p. 458.

[19] Brooke Foss Westcott, *The Gospel According to St. John* (James Clark & Co., 1958), p. 245.

[20] It is significant for this argument that in the Apocalypse Christ's
words are explicitly identified with the revelation of God. Revelation 1:2,
9; 12:17 and 20:4 equate the "testimony of Jesus Christ" with the "word
(or commandments) of God," both phrases appearing as synonymous epi-
thets for the one revelation given by God to men. And in Revelation
19:10 and 22:20 the testimony of Jesus is equated with the Scriptures,
with the Old Testament and presumably also with the Apocalypse itself,
which is presented to its readers as the revelation of Jesus Christ (1:1;
22:20). In these passages the phrase "of Jesus Christ" must be regarded
as a subjective genitive; thus, the testimony which Jesus gave, His revelation, as opposed to testimony about Him. Here as in the gospel there is
no indication of any conflict between the witness of Jesus, the words of
God which are spoken by Jesus, and Scripture, all three of which are to
be regarded as different ways of looking at a single, divine reality. For
this reason Jesus can speak in the gospel as one having authority, not on
His own authority as is emphasized in the Synoptics (Matt. 7:29), but
on the authority of the Father because His teaching is the teaching of
Scripture and of the Father who sent Him (7:16-18). In the Apocalypse
as in the gospel Jesus is thought of as the perfect revealer of the Father

and, for this reason, His spoken words are considered a perfect, although partial (16:12-15), revelation.

21 Dodd, *op. cit.*, p. 267.

22 C. K. Barrett, *The Gospel According to St. John* (S. P. C. K., 1962), p. 62 and Edwin Clement Hoskyns, *The Fourth Gospel* (Faber and Faber, 1961), pp. 136, 137.

23 Frederik Godet, *The Gospel of John*, I (Funk & Wagnalls, 1886), p. 290.

CHAPTER 4

1 Hans Freiherr von Campenhausen, *Die Idee des Martyriums in der alten Kirche* (Vandenhoeck & Ruprecht, 1964), pp. 38, 39 and Albert Vanhoye, "Témoignage et vie en Dieu selon le quatrième Évangile," *Christus*, 2 (1955), pp. 152-155.

2 Birger Gerhardsson, *Memory and Manuscript* (C. W. K. Gleerup, 1964), p. 213.

3 Nils Alstrup Dahl, however, holds that in the Jewish literature Israel was believed to have heard God's voice at Sinai and, in spite of Deuteronomy 4:12, to have seen his form there. Dahl refers to the Midrash Mekilta on Exodus 19:11 which comments: "This teaches that at that moment they saw what Isaiah and Ezekiel never saw," namely, a theophany — "The Johannine Church and History," *Current Issues in New Testament Interpretation*, ed. by William Klassen and Graydon F. Snyder (Harper & Row, 1962), p. 133.

4 John Calvin, *The Gospel According to John*, I (Eerdmans, 1956), pp. 215, 216; Frederik Godet, *The Gospel of John*, I (Funk & Wagnalls, 1886), p. 57; and Rudolf Bultmann, *Das Evangelium des Johannes* (Vandenhoeck & Ruprecht, 1962), pp. 199, 200.

5 C. H. Dodd, *Historical Tradition in the Fourth Gospel* (Cambridge, 1963), p. 288.

6 Alfred Loisy, *Le quatrième Évangile* (Alphonse Picard et Fils, 1903), p. 203.

7 Dodd, *op. cit.*, pp. 248-249. The same three-part schema has been outlined by Bernard, who calls attention to the fact that John presents it in a historical sequence of three consecutive days, "the first being the *announcement* of the Coming One, the second the *designation* of Jesus as He who was to come, and the third having as its consequence the *following* of Jesus by two of John's disciples" — *The Gospel According to St. John*, I (T. &. T. Clark, 1962), p. 34.

8 A helpful and illuminating emphasis upon the direct and supernatural character of prophetic revelation and upon the prophet himself as one who has been admitted to the councils of God and thus to a knowledge of his intentions has been provided by a series of studies by H. Wheeler Robinson and T. W. Manson on the theme "The Council of Yahweh." Robinson wrote the first of these studies (*Journal of Theological Studies*, 45 [1944], pp. 151-157) to balance the strictly psychological explanation of

prophetic inspiration by the suggestion that Old Testament references to the Council of Yahweh have a more literal meaning than has been generally supposed. He maintains that the prophet who appeals to such a council is claiming to have been included in God's formal decisions in regard to Israel and thus to possess information which is not and cannot be accessible to ordinary men. In *Inspiration and Revelation in the Old Testament* (Oxford, 1956), which appeared subsequent to the original statement of this thesis, the same author broadens the theme of God's council to speak of the Old Testament prophet being "absorbed into, and dominated by, the consciousness of being a direct spokesman of God to Israel and to the world" (p. 164) and of the prophetic function as that of one "who had been admitted into a higher fellowship, of which he became the earthly representative" (p. 169).

In a third but no less stimulating work ("Martyrs and Martyrdom," *Bulletin of the John Rylands Library,* 39 [1956, 57], pp. 463-484) T. W. Manson amplifies upon the views of Robinson in contrasting the Old Testament idea of the prophet with the conception of him as an enlightened commentator on public affairs which comes naturally to modern man. Manson notes that the deliverances of the prophets came out at irregular intervals and that the frequency and content of these utterances depended, not upon the prophet's wishes, but solely upon the grace and the purposes of God. According to Manson, the prophet found himself "listening to the discussions in Heaven between God and His immediate entourage on what was to be done with His people Israel. Consequently, the prophet never regarded himself as merely making acute guesses about what the future might hold, or intelligent forecasts of the probable behaviour of his human contemporaries. He always thought of himself as simply reporting decisions that had been taken at the top level, decisions about which he had firsthand information" (pp. 467, 468). According to this conception, the prophets appear as witnesses to what they have seen and heard in heaven. And Manson terms them "eyewitnesses and ministers of the word" (p. 469).

There is a sense, of course, in which the application of the term "eyewitness" to the prophets is inaccurate and in which the claim to such a witness may not be literally understood. But the appellation is not inept. And the emphasis which Robinson and Manson place upon the direct and supernatural character of the divine revelation to the prophets is certainly a correct one. It is much to the point that a similar experience of inspiration was not unknown to the rabbis even in the age of the Tannaim (the first to the fourth centuries A.D.) and that Jesus Himself, although in a highly exalted and uniquely definitive sense, also appears in John as the divinely commissioned messenger of God, as the one who has heard the heavenly message and who has come to earth that it might be heard by men.

9 Dodd, *op. cit.,* p. 299.

10 Karl Barth, *Church Dogmatics,* I, 2 (T. & T. Clark, 1963), pp. 120, 121.

11 C. H. Dodd, *The Interpretation of the Fourth Gospel* (Cambridge,

1963), p. 141. Cf. C. K. Barrett, *The Gospel According to St. John* (S. P. C. K., 1962), p. 63.

[12] Dodd, *The Interpretation of the Fourth Gospel*, p. 364.

[13] Karl Barth, *Der Christ als Zeuge* (Kaiser Verlag, 1934), pp. 5, 6; and Rudolf Bultmann, *Theology of the New Testament*, II (Scribners, 1955), p. 60.

[14] Campenhausen, *op. cit.*, p. 38.

[15] Norbert Brox, *Zeuge and Maertyrer* (Kösel-Verlag, 1961), pp. 73, 74 and 71.

[16] Rudolf Bultmann, *Jesus* (Deutsche Bibliothek, 1929), p. 180; *Theology of the New Testament*, II, p. 46; *Das Evangelium des Johannes*, p. 200.

[17] Charles Hodge, *Systematic Theology*, I (James Clark & Co. 1960), p. 636.

[18] Dodd, *Historical Tradition in the Fourth Gospel*, p. 297.

[19] Bultmann, *Theology of the New Testament*, II, pp. 44, 45.

[20] Dodd, *The Interpretation of the Fourth Gospel*, p. 329.

[21] Godet, *op. cit.*, II, pp. 121, 122 and Bernard, *op. cit.*, II, p. 321.

[22] Calvin, *op. cit.*, I, pp. 360, 361; Brooke Foss Westcott, *The Gospel According to St. John* (James Clark & Co., 1958), p. 140.

[23] Edwin Clement Hoskyns, *The Fourth Gospel* (Faber and Faber, 1961), pp. 347, 348; Adolf Schlatter, *Der Evangelist Johannes* (Calwer Verlag, 1960), p. 220; and Barrett, *op. cit.*, p. 291.

[24] Westcott, *op. cit.*, p. lxix.

[25] Numerous passages in Jewish documents illustrate the belief that the Torah is itself the source of life. Strack-Billerbeck provide a number of quotations, among them the following from the Siphre on Deuteronomy 32:2: "As rain is life for the world, so also are the words of Torah life for the world." Hoskyns draws attention to a similar statement from I Baruch 4:1, 2: "This is the book of the commandments of God and the Law that endureth for ever. All they that hold it fast are appointed to life; but such as leave it shall die." Hillel's words to the same effect are proverbial: "More flesh more worms; more wealth more care; more maidservants more lewdness; more menservants more thieving; more women more witchcraft; more Torah more life. . . . Whoso has gained a good name has gained it for himself; who has gained for himself words of Torah has gained for himself the life of the world to come" (Pirkē Aboth 2:8). Against this background Jesus wished to say that the study of the Scriptures in the formal manner of the Rabbis was not a guarantee of the life to come, as they believed. Christ is the life, not the Scriptures considered in themselves. Their true value lies in drawing men to Him. In searching for life only within the Torah the Jews perverted its intentions and misinterpreted its prophecies of Christ.

It is to be observed in addition, however, that a wider perspective must be given to this form of unbelief by the fact that in John's gospel a reference to the Jews is not exclusively nationalistic. John considers the Jewish people as a unit, but he looks upon that unit as a representative body of all men, of the world in its unbelief and opposition toward God. The appellation "Jew" is not opposed to Gentile, but to the Israel of God, the Church which is composed of all believing Jews and Gentiles. In speaking of the Jewish perversion of the law, therefore, John is actually carrying his analysis beyond the local situation of one particular people at one particular time in history to speak of the danger facing all men when they trust to the externals rather than to the reality, which is Christ, and when they count religion something to be possessed rather than the demand of God upon the human mind and consciousness.

26 R. H. Strachan, *The Fourth Gospel: Its Significance and Environment* (S. C. M., 1960), p. 175.

27 Godet, *op. cit.,* I, p. 490. Godet observes that this is the same thesis which Paul develops in Romans 2:6-10 and 26-29.

CHAPTER 5

1 Karl Heinrich Rengstorf, "*Apostellō, k. t. l.,*" *Theological Dictionary of the New Testament,* I (Eerdmans, 1964), pp. 398-447; *Apostolat und Predigtamt* (W. Kohlhammer Verlag, 1934), pp. 7-11.

2 Norbert Brox, *Zeuge und Maertyrer* (Kösel-Verlag, 1961), p. 46; cf. pp. 50-52.

3 Jean Bichon, "Le témoignage," *Foi et Vie,* 50 (1952), pp. 489-503; Emil Brunner, *Revelation and Reason* (Westminster, 1946), pp. 123-125; Marcus Barth, *Der Augenzeuge* (Evangelischer Verlag, 1946), p. 184; Robert P. Casey, "Martys," *The Beginnings of Christianity,* ed. by F. J. Foakes-Jackson and Kirsopp Lake, part I, vol. 5 (1933), note 5, pp. 30-37; Oscar Cullmann, "The Tradition," *The Early Church* (S. C. M., 1956), p. 71f.; and Karl Holl, "Der urspruengliche Sinn des Namens Maertyrer," *Gesammelte Aufsaetze zur Kirchengeschichte II, Der Osten* (1928), pp. 103-109 and "Pseudomartys," *Gesammelte Aufsaetze zur Kirchengeschichte* II, pp. 110-114.

4 Hermann Strathmann, "Die Entstehung und der Wortlaut (Text) des Neuen Testaments," *Das Neue Testament Deutsch,* I (Vandenhoeck & Ruprecht, 1963), p. 7.

5 Hans Lietzmann, *The Beginnings of the Christian Church* (Lutterworth, 1962), p. 67.

6 Dennis Nineham, "Eye-Witness Testimony and the Gospel Tradition," *Journal of Theological Studies,* N. S. 9 (1958), 13-25, 243-252; N. S. 11 (1960), 253-264.

7 Rudolf Bultmann, *Das Evangelium des Johannes* (Vandenhoeck & Ruprecht, 1962), pp. 374-401.

8 Cullman, *op. cit.,* p. 79.

9 Hoskyns finds every reason for affirming a strong belief in the apostolic authority and in the solidarity of the apostolic witness on the part of orthodox believers in *Greek-speaking, Greek-thinking,* proconsular Asia and

represented to all appearances independently by John, Polycarp, and Ignatius (*The Fourth Gospel,* Faber and Faber, 1961, pp. 96-106).

[10] Brooke Foss Westcott, *The Gospel According to St. John* (James Clark & Co., 1958), p. 298.

[11] Barth, *op. cit.,* p. 281.

[12] Oscar Cullmann, *Salvation in History* (Harper & Row, 1967), pp. 105, 106. Cullmann has developed the same theme in "The Tradition," pp. 59-75. Cf. Rengstorf, *Apostolat und Predigtamt,* pp. 33-37.

[13] Cullmann, "The Tradition," p. 73.

[14] *Ibid.,* p. 80.

[15] Frederik Godet, *The Gospel of John,* I (Funk & Wagnalls, 1886), p. 194.

[16] John Henry Bernard, *The Gospel According to St. John,* II (T. & T. Clark, 1958), p. 649.

[17] G. H. C. Macgregor, *The Gospel of John* (Hodder and Stoughton, 1959), p. 351.

[18] Hoskyns believes that the "we" of verse twenty-four is to be taken in the same sense as the occurrences of "we" throughout the gospel (1:14; I John 1:1-4); that is, to designate the "original apostles of the Lord, of whom the Beloved Disciple was one" (*op. cit.,* pp. 559, 560). This is an attractive possibility, especially in the light of the claim made in the present work that John places great importance on the verificational function of the apostolic witness, and Hoskyns' arguments for it are better than might be thought possible. Hoskyns maintains that chapter twenty-one is the natural conclusion of the gospel, not chapter twenty, in spite of the recommendation of the author in 20:30, 31, and adds that the so-called appendix is, therefore, from the same pen which wrote the body of the gospel. If this is true, as Westcott and others also believe, to deny that verses twenty-four and twenty-five are by the same author is to leave the gospel as it came from the evangelist without a conclusion. The supposition would then be that John himself composed the postscript, or the actual author writing in his name, and referred by the plural verb form to the combined witness of the apostles as he presumably also does in 1:14; 3:11 and I John 1:1-4. This argument has added support from the fact that the witness of the beloved disciple is referred to in the present ("This is the disciple who is bearing witness to these things," verse 24) and may therefore be presumed to be alive himself and to be the author of the closing attestation.

Despite the fact that this view accords well with the thesis earlier maintained in this study and is, therefore, in agreement with John's own conception of the apostolate, it is doubtful whether it can be accepted. If the author wrote the postscript, the identification of the author in this verse seems inexplicable in the light of the repression of the author's identity throughout the gospel. And it is a fatal objection that if the gospel itself was composed toward the end of the first Christian century and in Asia Minor, possibly in Ephesus as the tradition of Papias and Eusebius would lead one to expect, it is hard to see how enough of the members of the original apostolate could still be living and in contact with the aged apostle John to invest the "we" with any present and legitimate authority. Presumably John is the last of the apostles. And the whole tenor of the concluding verses would seem to be that his witness is now declared in the moment of the publication of the gospel to have an official and permanent authority. In this case the present tense of the author's witness ("the disciple who is bearing witness," verse 24) serves to indicate the vital continuity of his testimony which abides with an ever increasing relevance through his written word.

If John's authorship of the concluding verses of the gospel is rejected, the only remaining possibility is that the "we" of verse twenty-four represents the existence of an apostolic church, presumably composed of the Ephesian elders (and containing perhaps the presbyter John), capable of verifying the identity of the witness and of certifying that the gospel itself is a genuine composition from his hand.

[19] Oscar Cullmann, "A New Approach to the Interpretation of the Fourth Gospel," *The Expository Times*, 71 (1959), pp. 8-12, 39-43 and John A. T. Robinson, "The New Look at the Fourth Gospel," *Twelve New Testament Studies* (S. C. M., 1962), pp. 94-106.

[20] Bo Reicke, "Traces of Gnosticism in the Dead Sea Scrolls?" *New Testament Studies*, 1 (1955), pp. 137-141.

[21] A. M. Hunter, "Recent Trends in Johannine Studies," *Expository Times*, 71 (1959), p. 166.

[22] Robinson, *op. cit.*, pp. 98, 99.

[23] C. H. Dodd, *Historical Tradition in the Fourth Gospel* (Cambridge, 1963), p. 423.

[24] Burnett Hillman Streeter, *The Four Gospels* (Macmillan, 1961), pp. 417 f.

[25] C. H. Dodd, *The Interpretation of the Fourth Gospel* (Cambridge, 1963), p. 75.

[26] Robinson, *op. cit.*, p. 100.

[27] Oscar Cullmann, *Early Christian Worship* (S. C. M., 1962), p. 38; "Der johanneische Gebrauch doppeldeutiger Ausdruecke als Schluessel zum Verstaendnis des vierten Evangeliums," *Theologische Zeitschrift*, 4 (1948), pp. 360-372.

[28] Hoskyns, *op. cit.*, p. 85.

[29] Karl Barth, *Der Christ als Zeuge* (Kaiser Verlag, 1934), pp. 10, 12.

[30] Some writers have argued at this point that a distinction must be maintained between witness to the external revelation as a witness to the facts and witness to the internal revelation as a witness to one's opinion about the facts. Fact and opinion may differ, and the difference may be reflected in what has been called here response to the internal and response to the external revelation.

The important distinction between a witness as a witness to the facts and a witness as one who provides a moral or ethical evaluation of a person, an opinion witness, has been made with great clarity from Greek literature by Strathmann in the article for the Kittel *Theological Dictionary*

of the New Testament and plays an important role throughout in his interpretation of the texts. Aristotle's *Rhetoric* provides a natural point of
departure for Strathmann's exposition. According to Aristotle, a distinction must be drawn between natural and artificial, by which he means
technically developed means of proof; and each of these divisions must
be further analyzed to allow for testimony concerning an event as well as
testimony which deals with custom. The former is to be derived from
laws, formal evidence, torture, and oaths. The second case includes the
wisdom of oracles and proverbs and the judgment of people who have
distinguished themselves in the community. Thus, according to Aristotle,
witness divides itself into distinguishable classes in which, on the one
hand, inquiry is made into facts, externally observable, and, on the other
hand, into ethical judgments, expressions of moral convictions and personal
opinions.

The forensic distinction thus clearly made in the *Rhetoric* is found by
Strathmann in less formal settings throughout the writings of many Greek
authors and philosophers both before and after Aristotle. In illustration
of a testimony to the facts Strathmann cites instances in which the gods
are called as witnesses by affirmation or oath, cases in which a person has
been produced as an eye or ear witness of an event, and the transference
of the witness terminology to inanimate objects as to a prevailing state
or a condition. Such usage is prevalent in Homer, Pindar, Sophocles and
other authors. The second class of testimony is found by Strathmann
predominantly in Plato (and perhaps also, therefore, in Socrates) and in
the application of the substantive to the philosopher by Epictetus. In
Plato a chorus of young men, the Athenians, and the poet Theognis of
Megara are cited as witnesses to various truths.

In Epictetus one finds an example of the use of the witness terminology
to characterize the role of the philosopher in Stoic teaching. The philosopher, says Epictetus in the most extensive expression of the idea, appears in life as a witness summoned by God. "God says, 'Go you and
bear witness for me; for you are worthy to be produced by me as a
witness. . . .' What kind of witness do you bear for God? 'I am in sore
straits, O Lord, and in misfortune; no one regards me, no one gives me
anything, all blame me and speak ill of me.' Is this the witness that you
are going to bear, and is this the way in which you are going to disgrace
the summons which He gave you. . . ?" (*Discourses,* I, xxix, 47-49, Loeb
translation by W. A. Oldfather, Harvard, 1961). In other passages the
witness so conceived appears to be identical with the superior life of the
educated man (I, xxix, 56) and is directed on the part of God through
the philosopher toward the uninstructed masses (III, xxiv, 113; xxvi, 28).
Thus, Epictetus provides an example, not only of the concept of the philosopher witness, but equally important of the coexistence in one author
of the witness terminology used of a witness to the facts and of the same
terminology used of a witness to philosophical opinion.

The difficulty with this distinction, however, in spite of its general validity, is that it is often beside the point in dealing with the biblical material. Strathmann has implicitly recognized this difficulty in omitting the
distinction from his treatment of the Old Testament texts, but he terms

the distinction "fundamental" for an understanding of the use of the words in the New Testament. In defense of this position it is right to note that the distinction is sometimes helpful where the testimony of a person is concerned, and it must be frankly admitted that in one sense the testimony of the apostles and of other men is always to their personal persuasion that Jesus of Nazareth is indeed the Son of God. But even here the testimony to the opinion is only with difficulty separated from the witness to the facts — especially in Luke's characteristic restricting of the role of the witness to one who was in a position to have a special knowledge of the events concerning Jesus' life (Acts 2:22-32; 10:36-43; 13:23-31) — and in Christ's case the distinction is irrelevant. His witness is concerned with revelation, especially as the idea is developed in the Fourth Gospel. To some extent the situation is improved by Campenhausen's phrasing of the distinction as a witness to a thing or to a person (*Die Idee des Martyriums in der alten Kirche,* Vandenhoeck & Ruprecht, 1964, p. 33 ff.). But here again the point has little meaning when related to a religious witness, and Campenhausen would seem to oversimplify the matter when he presses the distinction to characterize the Lukan and Johannine modes of thought. Luke's witness is above all a witness to the facts. But Luke's factual witness cannot be separated from opinions about Christ's person — "You shall be *my* witnesses" (Acts 1:8). And John's personal witness is at the same time a witness to the facts. In the case of John particularly the religious truths are perceived by men precisely in the facts, and Christ's own witness transcends both opinion and fact in bearing testimony by word and deed to the great truths of the Christian revelation.

[31] Otto Michel, "Biblisches Bekennen und Bezeugen," *Evangelische Theologie,* 2 (1935), pp. 231-245. "The holy Scripture connects faith with speech. . . . No confession is possible without faith; but neither is faith possible without confession," p. 231. Cf. Hermann Diem, "Das Bekenntnis in der Kirche des Neuen Testaments," *Evangelische Theologie,* 1 (1934, 35), pp. 420-442. Diem adds that it is this confession which distinguishes between the world and the Christian congregation (p. 437).

CHAPTER 6

[1] Martin Luther, *The Small Catechism,* exposition of the third article; John Calvin, *Institutes of the Christian Religion* (Westminster, 1960), I, vii, 4; III, ii, 33.

[2] Oscar Cullmann, *Early Christian Worship* (S. C. M., 1962), p. 41; *Salvation in History* (Harper & Row, 1967), p. 250.

[3] Cullmann, *Early Christian Worship,* p. 42.

[4] Rudolf Bultmann, "Exkurs: Der Paraklet," *Das Evangelium des Johannes* (Vandenhoeck & Ruprecht, 1962), p. 539.

[5] Cullmann, *Early Christian Worship,* p. 44.

[6] *Ibid.,* p. 47.

[7] Brooke Foss Westcott, *The Gospel According to St. John* (James Clark & Co., 1958), p. 212.

[8] C. H. Dodd, *The Interpretation of the Fourth Gospel* (Cambridge, 1963), p. 414.

[9] John Henry Bernard, *The Gospel According to St. John*, II (T. & T. Clark, 1958), p. 497.

[10] C. K. Barrett, "The Holy Spirit in the Fourth Gospel," *Journal of Theological Studies*, N. S. 1 (1950), pp. 1-15, and *The Gospel According to St. John* (S. P. C. K., 1962), pp. 385, 386.

[11] Edwin Clement Hoskyns, *The Fourth Gospel* (Faber and Faber, 1961), p. 470.

[12] *Ibid.*, p. 469.

Appendix

[1] Eero Repo, *Der Begriff 'Rhema' im Biblisch-Griechischen: I, 'Rhema' in der Septuaginta* (1951), pp. 59-62.

[2] Strack-Billerbeck, *Kommentar zum Neuen Testament aus Talmud und Midrasch*, II (C. H. Beck, 1961), pp. 302-333 and George Foot Moore, *Judaism in the First Centuries of the Christian Era: The Age of the Tannaim*, I (Harvard, 1962), p. 417. For the phrase *memra Adonai* see Strack-Billerbeck, II, pp. 319-329.

[3] C. K. Barrett, *The Gospel According to St. John* (S. P. C. K., 1962), p. 128.

[4] Cf. Edwin Clement Hoskyns, *The Fourth Gospel* (Faber and Faber, 1961), p. 159.

[5] C. H. Dodd, *The Interpretation of the Fourth Gospel* (Cambridge, 1963), p. 265.

[6] Vinzenz Hamp, *Der Begriff 'Wort' in den aramaeischen Bibeluebersetzungen* (Neuer Fiber-Verlag, 1938), p. 193.

INDEX OF SUBJECTS

Dualism, 132

Early Church, 36-38
Election, 139, 150, 151
Eliezer Ben Jacob, 109
Enoch, I and II, 160
Ephraim, 132
Epictetus, 59, 179
Erasmus, 125
Eusebius, 166
Evidence, 75-77, 110-113
Eyewitness testimony, 17, 129-131, 174
Eyewitness, the, 135
Eyewitness tradition, 134, 136
Ezra, IV, 160

Faith, 146, 148-151
and reason, 98
provoked by signs, 99
Fall of Jerusalem, 36
False witnesses, 17, 168
Fourth Gospel,
authorship of, 123-136; its (Aramaic) background, 131-135; topography, 132, 133; unique in content, 133, 134; unites facts and faith, 135

Geffcken, Johannes, 165
Gerhardsson, Birger, 78, 173
Glory,
of God, 34; of Jesus Christ, 33, 55
Gnosticism, 37, 38, 69, 131, 132, 162
Gnostic Redeemer myth, 169, 170
God,
as Father, 54; as a witness, 19, 26

Godet, Frederik, 72, 79, 103, 110, 125, 171, 173, 175-177
Gospel (*kerygma*), 66
Guenther, Ernst, 166

Hamp, Vinzenz, 161, 163, 181
Healing, 92, 93
Hellenistic Christianity, 131, 132
Hillel, 49, 175
Hodge, Charles, 98, 99, 175
Holl, Karl, 115, 165, 166, 176
Holtzmann, H. J., 117
Holy Spirit,
Christ's advocate, 144, 145, 153-158; advocate of the disciples, 157; agent of revelation, 70, 143-158; Comforter, 145, 156; convicts of sin, 156-158; given to believers, 70; given to the disciples, 120; internal witness of, 138, 143-145; leads men to believe, 150, 153; ministers as Jesus Christ, 152; Paraclete, 151-158; sent by Jesus Christ, 152; Spirit of Truth, 61, 151, 152, 158; witness of, 27, 143-158
Homer, 15, 179
Hoskyns, Edwin Clement, 49, 69, 104, 135, 156, 158, 171, 175-178, 181
Huber, Hugo, H., 41, 45, 169, 170
Human witness,
by exemplary conduct, 141, 142; to the facts, 137, 138; mission, 140-142; re-

sponse to revelation, 136-140
Human witnesses, listed, 26
Hunter, A. M., 132, 178

Incarnation, 161
Internal witness of the Spirit, 143-145
Irenaeus, 37
Isaiah, 104, 105

Jeremias, 54, 132
Jesus Christ,
authority of, 51, 52; brings the Kingdom, 51, 52; forgives sins, 50, 51; God's messenger, 40; his hour, 46, 52; Logos, 65, 72, 73; mediator of creation, 67; mediator of revelation, 41; messianic consciousness of, 44-49; object of revelation, 54-56, 73; pre-existent, 46, 67; Revealer, 32, 39-43; righteousness of, 157; self-knowledge, 26, 32, 44-49, 170, 171; sends the Holy Spirit, 152; sent by God, 39, 40; Son of God, 44, 45, 49; subordinate to the Father, 40, 41, 55; the Truth, 61-65; unique, 41, 46; witness of, 26; witnesses through the apostles, 121-123; words of, 40, 65-67; works of, 40
John the Baptist,
confessor, 88; forerunner, 82; lamp, 86; Nazarite, 85; not the Messiah, 83; outline

INDEX OF SCRIPTURE REFERENCES